A LOVE STORY...
WITH A
HAPPY ENDING

Dados Internacionais de Catalogação na Publicação (CIP)
(Câmara Brasileira do Livro, SP, Brasil)

Gikovate, Flávio
A love story – with a happy ending / Flávio Gikovate ;
translated by Alison Entrekin. – São Paulo: MG Editores, 2009.

Título original: Uma história do amor — com final feliz
ISBN 978-85-7255-063-5

1. Amor 2. Individualidade 3. Psicologia aplicada I. Título.

09-07351                                                        CDD-158

Índice para catálogo sistemático:

1. Amor : Psicologia aplicada     158

No part of this work may be reproduced or transmitted
in any form or by any means, electronic or mechanical,
including photocopying and recording, or by any
information storage or retrieval system without the prior
written permission of Summus Editorial unless such
copying is expressly permitted by federal copyright law.

# A LOVE STORY... WITH A HAPPY ENDING

Flávio Gikovate

Translated by Alison Entrekin

*A LOVE STORY... WITH A HAPPY ENDING*
Copyright © 2009 by Flávio Gikovate
All rights reserved by Summus Editorial

Translation: **Alison Entrekin**
Cover design: **Alberto Mateus**
Art and design: **Crayon Editorial**

**MG Editores**
Editorial departament:
Rua Itapicuru, 613 – 7º andar
05006-000 – São Paulo – SP
Brazil
Tel.: (55) (11) 3872-3322
Fax: (55) (11) 3872-7476
http://www.mgeditores.com.br
e-mail: mg@mgeditores.com.br

Printed in Brazil

# introduction

**This book tells the story** of love as it has been experienced by those who, like myself, have had to act as pioneers. Love has always been treated as something to be left to the artists, rather than submitted to the sharp scalpel of the sciences of the mind. I refuse to accept this and believe that in four decades of work — and personal experience — I have made significant progress.

My objective is clear: to help people better negotiate this terrain that has traditionally been a source of enormous suffering. I am a firm believer in the power of knowledge and it is my opinion that developing good hypotheses and looking to them for guidance goes a long way towards helping us progress with more confidence and less pain. We should always strive to grow, no matter what our age. Of course, young people probably have more to gain from reading this book, since they may be able to avoid some of the obstacles that older generations have had to face. They may be able to traverse in months — or a few years — a path that used to take, when successful, over a decade. This book offers a surprising new take on love and lays the foundations for intimate relationships that truly respect our growing

individual concerns. New ways of thinking are almost never in keeping with traditional feelings. Growth means re-establishing inner harmony, working from solid ideas. It is an arduous task, but I believe the effort will be fully rewarded.

Becoming familiar with the nuances surrounding the phenomenon of love is a fascinating adventure. Such a process, however, must be useful; it should serve individual growth and real progress toward happiness. Here you will find good answers to many of your concerns. This should inspire optimism in those who, while aware of the difficulties to be overcome, are able to glimpse the reward at the end of the journey.

# A Love Story... with a Happy Ending

# one

**Once upon a time** a cell came into being as the result of the fusion of two others. Then this process reversed and it began to divide. After only a few weeks, there were millions of cells. Then they began to differentiate themselves from one another, each group following its own script: some gave origin to arms and legs; others to a torso and different organs. A handful of cells split in a peculiar way and generated neurons, together forming a nervous system, which established its centre in the cranium.

After another few weeks, this organism began to function in a rudimentary (but very interesting) manner. Without breathing, it took nourishment from the blood it received through a cord connected to its mother and eliminated its waste in the liquid in which it was immersed and which purified itself automatically. It suddenly began to move in a way that could be felt by the host (the mother). From the stories I have heard, this seems to be the moment when the penny really drops for mothers, who realize they are carrying a living being inside them.

This is how our story begins, just like the story of love. We didn't exist, and then, at some stage in our

intra-uterine stay, we did. We weren't and then we were! Some of the processes involved in this phase are known, while others are unknown and mysterious. No one knows if we will one day understand it completely. Scientists believe we will. People with a more religious outlook don't. I'm not sure where to position myself on the matter and, fortunately, don't have to.

I am happy I am not required to pass judgement on the precise moment in which a "non-being" becomes a "being", since from this moment on any act against it must be treated as homicide. Some believe that this happens on day one; others, that it takes place when the foetus is more developed (at the end of the third month of pregnancy); yet others think that "being" is defined by the first moment of consciousness.

I am convinced that our brains, initially devoid of information, categorically record the latter portion of our uterine stay. It is a positive record, mostly involving a feeling of harmony (although there may be some discomfort, especially in the last few weeks of this "symbiosis"). **I believe it was this harmonious record that gave rise to the biblical idea (Genesis) that life begins in paradise: a calm place, where nothing extraordinary happens, food is abundant, one lives without thinking, and the most one must do is yawn and stretch.**

The more I think about it, the more perplexed I get when I try to understand the path taken by those who have undergone this kind of introspection. Aristophanes says the same thing in Plato's *The Symposium*. He says

that, originally, we were dual and had four arms, four legs, two torsos, and two heads. A CAT scan of a woman late in pregnancy would be confirmation that this "dual creature" actually exists. Exceptional or inspired individuals have, it seems, been able to vicariously capture the first things the brain recorded while still in the womb. The foetus is in harmony and its brain develops a feeling that corresponds to this state, which seems to stem from its being connected to its mother, perhaps even part of her. **They are a single entity.**

**The brain only does what is essential. So, if there are no problems, the only record is of serenity.** Since it knows no other state, it doesn't get bored by the fact that nothing happens, which will later be unbearable. In this context, mother and child feel cosy. **I think this is the most primitive and simple manifestation of the complex phenomenon of love: a feeling of completeness (experienced more clearly by the mother, since she is also familiar with discomfort) originating from a state experienced as fusion with another human being.**

I reaffirm my belief that the feelings derived from this sensation remain in the empty brain; they are our first mental record. Semi-conscious life begins, and very nicely at that.

**Despite the apparently** positive beginning, the fact that our first mental record is a feeling of completeness is problematic, because later experiences are compared with it and rarely feel as soothing. They may be rich and interesting, but are hardly ever as harmonious. The most serious thing is that what follows this feeling of completeness is extraordinarily dramatic: suddenly, the membrane containing the amniotic fluid and foetus bursts and the painful process of labour begins. It is our big bang[1].

**Babies are born crying and in a state of panic. Their faces are a picture of desperation, which is to be expected, seeing as they have gone from wonderful to downright terrible. It is impossible to imagine a more drastic transition.** Those who watch a birth smile, joyfully acknowledging the arrival of a new being. Meanwhile, the baby cries and cries. Current efforts to reduce birth-related stress are more than called for, but they are palliative measures that can only ease a little of a newborn's real drama.

---

1 I sometimes wonder about the correlation between our birth and what astronomers describe as the birth of the universe.

The more I think about it, the more convinced I become that birth is the biggest and most traumatic experience of our lives. We are flung from paradise straight into a torture camp! Little by little the desperation dissipates and we realize, thanks to the care we receive, that we are not totally abandoned and that his new state — capable of generating a terrible feeling of forsakenness — can be eased by the helpful presence of our mother (or a substitute), who is always (or almost always) ready to alleviate all kinds of physical discomfort. It's all new and not at all pleasant, since we have never felt hunger, thirst, or cold before, or uncomfortable excrement in our nappies. Before, we didn't even have to breathe, as we received previously oxygenated blood in the uterus.

**Birth has always received the treatment given to "facts of life", which may explain why the pain and traumatic experiences involved have been overlooked. It is curious to think that facts of life can be brutally traumatic; but it is also strange to overlook them just because they are "natural".** The pain of women in childbirth attracted medical attention long before the pain that babies feel. In the mid-$20^{th}$ century, people began to talk about painless births for mothers — which resulted in an enormous increase in the number of Caesarean sections. Some decades later, gynaecologists realized it might be a good idea to pay a little more attention to the suffering of babies, who should be born smiling (which is impossible).

I hope that this century psychology finally takes a serious interest in the subject, which I have been reflecting on since 1980. Notwithstanding honourable exceptions (among which the extraordinary Otto Rank, author of *The Trauma of Birth*, published in the early 20th century[2]), most psychoanalysts are still much more interested in the Oedipal complex and other events that come later.

Studies in neurophysiology show that major traumatic experiences leave almost indelible marks, which are somehow recorded physically in the central nervous system. There are thus physical and emotional marks. People who have lived through times of war and concentration camps, or who have survived fires, terrorist attacks, or natural disasters — of the many traumatic events that can befall us — can go for reasonably long periods of time without remembering these painful situations. But from time to time the memories come flooding back as strong as ever, as if the events had taken place only yesterday. Traumas leave marks and influence the lives of almost everyone who has experienced them.

**We cannot, therefore, continue to neglect the trauma of birth, the first and greatest of all**, which catches us completely unprepared, dependent, and fragile. It will be responsible for many relevant aspects of our future, especially those I discuss in the pages to come. **Another important consideration is that this is some-**

---

**2** The German edition of this book, *Das Trauma der Geburt*, was published in 1924. I consulted the English-language edition published by Basic Books, New York, in 1952.

thing that takes place on the frontier between what is innate, purely biological, and what happens to us as a life experience, inevitable and universal. It is not, however, part of our genetic arsenal. **Nor is it a permanent, inevitable phenomenon from the point of view of science and technology.** If, in the future, we are able to generate foetuses in glass incubators (we are not far from it), and if they are able to remain there for more than the nine months of uterine gestation, and if they are able to observe their surroundings without having to "be born" (leave the incubator), and if they can be born and unborn (return to the incubator from time to time), we may come to know beings who are devoid of the trauma of birth. But can they accurately be called human beings?

# 3
three

**The only resource** we have to try to understand what goes on in babies' minds is observation. They cry and make jerky movements, giving us the impression that they feel unprotected, lost, threatened, weak, and defenceless against the world around them. They look forsaken, and we assume it is how they feel. Everything suggests that what is going on in their minds is horrible. When, as adults, we find ourselves in situations that bear some resemblance to that of babies (being wheeled on a stretcher into an operating theatre, or lost in an unknown city in a country whose language we don't speak, etc.), we are overcome by a painful feeling of forsakenness.

What seems to reduce a baby's suffering? Being cradled by his mother (or another adult substitute). When he is in her arms breastfeeding or being bottle-fed, he appears to feel something that may be reminiscent of intrauterine life. **Previously protected inside his mother's belly, he is now cradled outside her.** There are many discomforts, all new and unexpected (when compared to its situation prior to birth), and all have to do with physiological functions that used to be resolved without any disruption to the peace and quiet of foetal life. There are uncomfortable nappy-rashes; air ingested during breastfeeding that requires a whole series of burping manoeuvres; not to mention colicky tummies, minor infections, earaches, etc.

**Being in the world instead of in our mothers' bellies is undoubtedly a change for the worse,** at least in this phase of our lives. Caring for newborns is intensive and goes on day and night, leaving mothers (especially more anxious or inexperienced ones) exhausted. When a mother finally works out why her baby is crying and alleviates both his physical and emotional suffering, he sleeps serenely. He feels comforted, and this seems to be his only true pleasure in his first few weeks of life.

**Should a mother have to be away from her baby for a few minutes — which is inevitable — and some kind of discomfort wakes her precisely at this moment, he will start crying again, and the terrifying feeling of pain, vulnerability, and forsakenness will return.** Even the most attentive (and well assisted) mothers are unable to prevent all moments of suffering. **When successfully resolved, the feeling of cosiness is reinstated.** Neonatal life seems to oscillate between despair and overcoming it, which leads to cosiness. This will inevitably be interrupted again by some form of discomfort, which will bring back the feeling of despair, which will again be resolved and restore the feeling of peace and equilibrium.

Newborns thus live in the domain of pain, and their only pleasure is derived from its end (a kind of negative pleasure, because it is a remedy for suffering). When babies aren't crying they are sleeping, and vice versa. (All of this, of course, is in the very beginning.)

**The person responsible for easing a baby's pain and restoring equilibrium is the one special (increasingly familiar) person whose simple presence always seems to bring good news. There is no doubt that for a baby his mother is everything!** He will not be able to survive without her, as she is his reason for living[3]. He nourishes a special, growing feeling for her. He wants to be near her all the time, snuggled up in her arms — the best place in the world and his greatest pleasure.

**I define love based on these considerations, as the feeling babies have for their mothers, who make them feel cosy and save them from abandonment.** Love is thus what we feel for the person who gives us the negative pleasure resulting from the end of the pain of forsakenness. Our adult love lives are not very different. I believe that, at least in part, our adult relationships repeat this early experience. Because we are not in the habit of trying to resolve feelings of forsakenness on our own, we go looking for mother-substitutes, who will have the mission of making us feel cosy throughout our adults lives.

---

**3** It is curious to think that these lines were deliberately taken from adult lovers' discourse.

four

**The weeks** go by and babies' periods of sleepiness grow shorter. Their motor skills improve and they are able to lift their heads, then sit up. Now awake, they are stimulated by their environment: people go past, they are taken outside for fresh air, they are intrigued by the sounds of rattles and other toys, which may also have flashing lights. They become acquainted with more and more objects, places, and people, with whom they gradually become familiar. They smile at the people they recognize (including their fathers, who only really enter the story here), and this is a sign of satisfaction and cosiness. **New is scary; familiar is soothing.** (Are we not like this throughout life, although we complain of boredom and the monotony of routine?)

The human brain is privileged, such that babies record everything and acquire an increasing amount of information, including words (sounds with fixed, specific meanings). The maturing of the peripheral nervous system, bones, and muscles allows babies to start crawling and, around the end of their first year of life, they hesitantly take their first few steps. They advance both physically and in the accumulation of data in the brain

— which I like to compare to a computer operating system. Little by little, our innate equipment is activated by a fledgling application — a memory program that allows it to amass information (which will gradually be connected and cross-referenced to other data).

Babies start to realize that they are separate entities to their mothers. Everything suggests that until now they have seen themselves as extensions of their mothers, as if their uterine state were still the norm. **Some authors refer to what happens at the end of a baby's first year of life as "psychological birth", an appropriate name because it indicates the beginning of self-awareness, that is, its true birth.**

This period coincides with efforts to discover their own physical limits, i.e., their bodies. Getting to know things means looking at them, putting them in their mouths, touching them. **Suddenly, there is a surprise: touching certain parts of their bodies provokes a curious and very enjoyable sensation, a pleasant tingling.** Later we will call these parts of the body erogenous zones, which essentially correspond to the genitals and the outside orifice of the anus. Babies tend to touch these pleasure-generating regions again and again. Most people continue to do so throughout childhood, adolescence, and even their adult lives.

**Thus, the sensation that we call sexual arousal first appears as a personal phenomenon, in other words, without the participation of another person.** It is a positive pleasure (so-named because it doesn't arise as a

consequence of the end of pain, as is the case with negative pleasure). First the child was in a state of equilibrium, and then, through touch, began to feel something that took it from stage zero to a pleasant, positive zone.

**This sexual arousal is personal, and it is called autoeroticism because it doesn't depend on anyone else, not even one's mother. It is arousal (a positive pleasure), not peace (a negative pleasure). On the other hand, the love a child feels for its mother depends on her very existence! Love is thus an interpersonal phenomenon par excellence. This being the case, love is a negative, interpersonal pleasure, while sex is a positive, personal pleasure.**

It is amazing how such different things, arising from our very first experiences, have been treated as if they were part of the same process, the same instinct (this word is used a lot, although I have yet to find a precise definition for it). Elementary mistakes in such relevant, basic areas can only give rise to ideas that are harmful to the quality of our adult lives.

five

**It is possible** that sexual arousal from the manipulation of erogenous zones reinforces the idea taking shape in a baby's mind that he is a separate being, rather than part of his mother. This is coupled with important advances in motor skills that allow him to walk, as well as mental progress that enables him to begin to formulate his first words. By the end of his second year, he can walk alone and put together comprehensible phrases, he has some sphincteral control, and is already brimming with tastes, desires, and "opinions" about various aspects of day-to-day life.

Watching children in this phase is extremely revealing. When they arrive in an unknown place with their mothers, they will, as a rule, feel threatened by the new and won't let go of their protectors. Little by little, they will feel more comfortable with the place and, at some stage, will want down from their mother's safe embrace. They are confident enough to begin the task of "exploring" . Touching everything in sight and putting things in their mouths, they use all of their senses to get to know the peculiarities of the place, especially things they have never seen before.

Different tastes cause them to smile or make faces. They try to throw objects and assess their weight. They try to discover how things work. When trying to understand, for example, how a music box (which plays music when its lid is open and stops playing when it is closed) works, they open and close it over and over, then finally smile from ear to ear with the self-satisfaction of one who has discovered something exceptional.

**Babies discover, always with the same satisfaction, how to open and close doors, remove sweet wrappers, and rock rocking chairs. Their learning-related pleasure is obvious[4].** They amass data with their increasingly active software and, with the passing months, are able to play with growing creativity and imagination. They watch films produced for their age group and are delighted by the images, songs, and stories that they understand more and more.

**In all of these cases, they are behaving like autonomous individuals, exercising their fledgling individuality and, in the way they organize the information they are gathering, forming their identity. They begin to acquire their own way of thinking and behaving.** They find satisfaction (in addition to that of an erotic nature) far from their mothers and regardless of their presence.

---

**4** This is an important point, since there are countless individuals who, as the years go by, lose the natural, innate pleasure related to learning. They become apathetic, indecisive, bored teenagers and adults, who can only be entertained passively by watching TV or talking to funny people. They often end up "killing" their boredom with alcohol and other drugs.

The pleasures related to learning are also positive, because they don't depend on prior suffering. **The most important point here is that their mothers are no longer their only source of satisfaction.**

I have described above what happens when everything is going well. But if a child slips, falls, and feels pain, she will cry and run to her mother for comfort (an important negative pleasure), which attenuates the feeling of forsakenness and insecurity that come flooding back and make her stop whatever she was doing — no matter how pleasurable it was. As soon as the pain has passed and she is calm again, she leaves her mother's protective embrace and continues her exploratory expedition, which is fun and stimulating. If her mother gets up to go to the bathroom, for example, she will drop everything and run to be with her. **All this, of course, is what happens when the baby trusts that her mother will comfort her (which, fortunately, is true in most cases). The more insecure she feels about the constancy of her "safe port", the more she will cling to her mother's apron strings, afraid of venturing away and being abandoned.** All children will, of course, feel some kind of uncertainty, since their mothers cannot be present to rescue them in every single moment of discomfort. At night, for example, babies cry and sometimes they are not immediately tended to. This is fine, because no one can be omnipresent. Mothers

just have to be "good enough" (Winnicott[5]) to avoid more serious problems related to these initial and ever-so fundamental ties (Bowlby[6]).

---

[5] Winnicott, D. W. *Home is where we start from: essays by a psychoanalyst.* New York: W. W. Norton & Company, 1986.
[6] Bowlby, J. *Attachment.* New York: Basic Books, 98. [Attachment and Loss, v. 1.]

six

**Our earliest moments** of life are punctuated by feelings of defencelessness and cosiness, and our minds are practically empty; our only dilemmas are related to discomfort and the presence, or not, of the maternal figure who knows how to alleviate them. With the development of motor skills and growing competence in the use of the brain's potential, individuality and a sense of identity begin to form. Individuality is related to a range of actions and thoughts, as well as autoerotic pleasures. **The mother — and the love her child feels for her — means peace, while individuality means action and entertainment of all kinds. Young children love their mothers and need them when they feel insecure, but they love to play and have fun at a distance. Therein lies our first big dilemma: love versus individuality.** Staying in their mothers' arms means giving up playing; while playing often means being away from their mothers. It isn't always possible to reconcile the two, nor it is always easy to decide which is best. At any rate, it is clear that love won't provide the action and entertainment inherent in exercising one's individuality.

At times, love may seem somewhat tedious compared to games or the cartoons on TV[7].

Children continue to be strongly attached to their mothers and need them close (perhaps not so close that they are always within eyeshot) for many years. The love versus individuality dilemma manifests clearly at around the age of 7 or 8, when children go to spend weekends at cousins' or friends' houses. They play and have fun all day long and barely remember their mothers even exist. But at bedtime, when the action is over and they find themselves in bed alone, in a strange place, surrounded by people who, though familiar, are not their parents, they start to cry and want their mothers.

The situation can sometimes be a little embarrassing and unexpected. As well as being a time for rest, nights are always more frightening. The unoccupied mind is assailed by an unpleasant sensation. It is despair, now more similar to the adult variety. The remedy? Maternal comfort! How many parents haven't had to go rescue their desperate children on nights when they expected to have some fun of their own? **As the years go by, it becomes more and more obvious that advances in individuality don't make the desire for cosiness disappear — sometimes it doesn't diminish at all. This observation is curious, especially if we consider that practical needs diminish a lot** (by the age of 12 or 13, pre-adoles-

---

[7] The same is true of adult life, where many people wrongly expect their romantic partner to entertain them and grow frustrated and bored with the lack of action of marital life.

cents are perfectly capable of looking after themselves; the Jewish coming of age takes place at 13). **In other words, the end of a child's practical dependence on its parents doesn't have an emotional equivalent!** While babies love their mothers because they are unable to conceive of themselves as individuals and depend on them for everything, the disappearance of these two variables does not dramatically change the feeling that we are just half of something and that we are only "complete" when this symbiosis is recreated. **We enjoy our time away from our beloved mother when we are occupied, entertained with individual matters. When we are at rest, we once again feel the "hole", a symbol of incompleteness, a kind of scar left by our earliest experiences.** The practical dependence is gone, but the emotional one (in no way related to survival), established in our first years of life, is still strong and shows no sign of abandoning us. The phenomenon doesn't seem at all logical.

It really appears to be a conditioned reflex, fruit of the traumatic end of the uterine connection. **It seems we always want to return to the womb, to be unborn. This should not be treated as the be-all and end-all, the best thing we can experience during our time on Earth. It is a problem to be solved, not something to be worshipped in verse and prose.** It wouldn't be such a serious problem if it weren't for the fact that our so-called adult loves reproduce the same dynamics: the desire to exercise one's individuality at the same time as wanting to have one's romantic partner nearby. Our lovers have their own individuality that wants to be exercised and they also want their romantic partner nearby! The struggle for power, for one to be more "in charge" than the other but to be in sync at all times, is part of the everyday life of most couples. Those who give in don't always do so without resentment, such that as fighting and eroded feelings are almost always par for the course.

seven

**One of the most difficult** things for people who work with the subject of love is the plethora of ready-made "formulas" that people learn and trot out as if they were absolute, irrefutable truths. Many inevitably get upset (somewhat irrationally) when one tries to take a more critical look at this emotion. It is as if you are committing heresy, a terrible sin. An old catchphrase holds that one must first love oneself before they can love another. Quite the contrary to the biblical expression "love thy neighbour as thyself."

It is an extremely complex matter and I hope to examine, little by little, all of its nuances. One is that people who apparently "love themselves" are more extroverted and practice self-promotion; as a rule, they are selfish and incapable of truly loving others. Shyer people who know they have lower self-esteem are the ones who surrender more fully to romantic love. It would seem, thus, that what we actually practice is the opposite of what the "formula" preaches.

**When one is more familiar with my whole line of thinking, it becomes clear that my disagreement is more radical: it isn't possible to love oneself!** I have come to this conclusion because of the way I define love: the feeling we have for those who make us feel peaceful and cosy. Unless we are able to feel peace and cosiness by the very fact of being in our own company, it is impossible to love oneself; and, if we could, we'd have to ask ourselves, "Why love someone else — what's in it for me?" Love is, in my opinion, a strictly interpersonal phenomenon, such that it cannot be reduced to the personal formula of "love thyself".

Love needs to be properly understood as a feeling. If we use the term as a synonym for self-esteem, we are making a big mistake. **Self-esteem has to do with value judgments, not feelings. It is a kind of rating that we give ourselves — generally, lower than it should be. Love, in its original version (what a child feels for its mother) is visceral, automatic, and has to do with uterine symbiosis. Love has an object. Self-esteem is rational and a form of self-assessment.**

If we take a close look at the distinction I make between sex and love, we will see that sex is indeed a personal phenomenon. In other words, self-arousal (not to be mistaken for self-lust) is present from the end of our first year of life. We humans have a capacity for individual, solitary sexual arousal. From the age of 6 or 7 on, we can become aroused simply by being admired by others (unidentified and without any sentimental importance): this is an important key to understanding people's private and social lives and is called "vanity".

**Flávio Gikovate**

**In short, we do harbour something important, but it isn't self-love. Rather, it is sexual arousal derived from the stimulation of erogenous zones or exhibitionism.** The idea of self-love (the narcissism of psychoanalytic theory) has given rise to many misconceptions due to the fact that sex and love are not treated as distinct (one of the pillars of the same theory). In my opinion, there is no such thing as self-love or self-lust; rather, there is autoerotism — the capacity for self-arousal.

**Children have contact** with other children from an early age. Relationships are simple and determined above all by circumstance: siblings, cousins, neighbours, classmates, and their parents' friends' children. At this stage in life, there is little discrimination, such that it is rare for them to show a clear preference for a particular person. This remains so until the age of 6.[8]

Thanks to the sophistication of logic, derived from the growing volume of information amassed in memory, children's personalities start becoming better defined from the age of 6, and they start to demonstrate clearer preferences for particular people. They like to play with some children more than others and get irritated by certain attitudes in others. They want to spend time with some and avoid those with whom they don't share any affinity. They talk at length and more sincerely with one or two friends, and this intimacy starts defining a new kind of bond, formed via the intellect: they are at home in their company because they think they are under-

---

[8] Children nowadays are intellectually stimulated from a very early age and with a hitherto unprecedented intensity. They demonstrate certain kinds of behaviour at ages much younger than they did, say, forty years ago.

stood by like-minded people, which makes them feel less alone in the world!

**We are looking at another remedy for the feeling of forsakenness. While love is the peace derived from the physical warmth a child feels in its mother's arms, the emotion of friendship is a more abstract form of cosiness, stemming from the fact that the child feels understood, not judged, part of a unit of similar people (which could perfectly well have more than two). Love is, as we know, a negative pleasure; but friendship is essentially positive in nature. The pleasure that comes from exchanging ideas is intense, even when there isn't any prior suffering.** Friendship is not devoid of negative pleasure, since we turn to our friends in times of pain. This is because we trust them and are comfortable talking about our problems with them.

**Love is physical cosiness, while friendship is intellectual cosiness.** Children — and later teenagers and adults — miss their friends (who can be many, although they tend to have a favourite, or "best" friend), but not with the same desperation that they miss their mothers and their later substitutes. We don't like it when our best friend is close to other people, even when they are also our friends. Jealousy exists, but it is much less intense than what we feel for our mothers and their substitutes. Jealousy is an important subject, which I will discuss as I go.

Friendship gains extraordinary strength in puberty and early adolescence. The arrival of adult sexuality is a

shock and has a great impact on the psychology of teenage boys and girls. The equilibrium — almost always somewhat precarious — between love and individuality is upset. With the passing years individuality tends to gain more and more space, and this is reinforced by the full expression of eroticism (until now always on the opposite side of love). The awareness of what adult life is and its vicissitudes also seems to propel young people towards a more radical break with their original emotional ties.

Many young people start clashing with other family members and act rudely, ostensibly pulling away from them: they dress in ways that will displease them, lock themselves in their rooms, barely speak to the very people they used to look up to, listen to strange music at barely tolerable volumes, etc. They become "rebels" who always think the opposite to what their parents think. They try to shape their individuality by going against everything they have experienced and learned. This is, of course, an effort to assert their individuality rather than a victory: those who are truly individuated don't need to rebel against anything, much less rudely! Many parents understand what is going on with their kids because they remember going through similar phases, while other appear not to have such good memories.

**In practice, this cooling of relationships with family members takes place as they grow closer to their friends.** They abandon their original nucleus and organize themselves in other groups of their own, whose members are going through similar experiences and dilemmas and finding similar solutions, at least superficially. They form tribes, the rebels who want to be different to their parents, who want to be original and attract peoples' attention — the most characteristic manifestation of vanity. Since they can't bear the pain of loneliness (which caused them to feel desperate in the past), an inevitable state for someone truly different to all other human beings, they bond with other people who are "different", forming a tribe of equals. **They are different to "others" (which stimulates their vanity) and equal to one another (which gives them a feeling of cosiness).**

Strong manifestations of adult sexuality (among other yearnings) demand increasing distinction, which reinforces the individualism that causes young people to grow away from their families. This distinction, a requirement of eroticism, leads to feelings of loneliness, whose pain is diminished by forming groups of friends with things in common. **Love is weakened; individuality, strengthened. The pain of forsakenness is only lessened by groups of friends in this first phase of adolescence. This victory of individuality is temporary and partial.**

nine

**In spite of teenagers' increasing** self-sufficiency, the "final victory" of individuality over love doesn't usually take place. Adult sexuality (in addition to reinforcing individuality by underlining vanity) prompts them couple to, generally with members of the opposite sex, which can give rise to a kind of attraction that is not merely sexual. This isn't always easy to see, especially in men, since they retreat when their desire has been satisfied, such that their individuality tends to take over again.

As the years go by, groups of friends tend to drift apart, as members go their separate ways. It happens at a time when young people are much more autonomous. A yearning for cosiness derived from a bond with someone special is suddenly reborn. Even when we barely know the person we have chosen, we start to nurture feelings for them that are similar to what we felt for our mothers. It is love, showing clear signs that it wasn't really dead, but, hibernating, cocooned somewhere in our subjectivity.

Why does this happen? Why do we not continue down the path of total independence (which has been our objective ever since we could think for ourselves)?

What can explain this radical backswing of the pendulum towards that which appeared to have been overcome and resolved?

It is important to note that this reversal wasn't inevitable, a result of our biology. It didn't — or doesn't — have to be like that. Something similar can be observed in dogs: they can live alone on the streets or they can live with human beings and become extraordinarily attached to them. In other words, I think our biology is unbiased here and that other factors, of a psychological and social nature, can have a strong influence on what happens to us.

**I believe that we still retain important memories and conditioning stemming from our childhood experiences that can have a great influence on our adult lives — much more than we would like or is convenient. The appearance of adult sexuality participates in this process in two different ways. One is because some people seem capable of "hypnotizing" us with their erotic appeal and awaken a desire for greater and more constant intimacy, which increases the risk of emotional attachment (not always entirely appropriate). The other has to do with the fact that sexual arousal is very nice, but incredibly solitary — especially at the moment of orgasm, when the other person disappears, even in masturbatory fantasies; the all-too-familiar feeling of forsakenness can be unbearable and prompt people to seek solutions that are repetitions of childhood ones.**

We also should not underestimate cultural influence, since the families we come from belong to a social order

in which reproduction requires a stable coupling between a man and a woman. The romantic aspects of relationships between adults are also transmitted to us through the exchange of caresses that we see in films and on TV (in addition, of course, to what we see around us in our day-to-day lives). The reappearance of this yearning for love at 15 or 16 years of age is highly complex, and I won't discuss it at length here. **The fact is that love comes flooding back at this stage. It reappears with its original characteristics, similar to those of the original mother-child relationship. It doesn't take on the characteristics typical of our earlier friendships. It returns in its most regressive version: lovers' desire for fusion!**

The dilemma between the desire for a feeling of cosiness born of intimacy with someone special and our yearning for individuality also returns in all its strength. **While love reappears in its original, primitive version, individuality has advanced a lot with the passing years: as well as being able to resolve almost all practical matters on their own, young people have also already formed more solid and consistent thought systems and have much clearer points of view.** These points of view will continue to morph quickly over the next few years, but they are experienced at any given moment as consistent and definitive.

Individuality is also highly reinforced by sexuality (to which it has always been connected). This is because of the exhibitionist nature of vanity, arousal itself, and ever-present desires; these, as a rule, don't have a clear-

cut object — arousal or desire manifest in many different circumstances, tripped off by different people who are almost never relevant in other aspects.

**The dilemma thus reappears in its most radical version: individuality on the one side, romantic love and desire for fusion on the other, both very strong.** The only way fusion wouldn't threaten a person's individuality is if lover and loved one were identical, which is impossible. So, how to resolve the dilemma? By relinquishing one or the other? This usually isn't the best solution, nor is it terribly long-lived, since we soon begin to yearn for the thing that we have given up.

**Our sophisticated, ingenious minds generally resort to subtle manoeuvres to try to resolve dualities of this kind. One of them is to transfer one side to the sphere of the imagination. The most common situation is for love to pass over into this realm and be experienced only in fantasy, while individuality continues to reign in everyday life.** Young people around the age of 15 have crushes on people close or distant, neighbours or film and rock stars. The condition is clear: their feelings must be unrequited! The best thing is for the object of this love not to be aware of what is going on in the subjectivity of the one who loves them. At the slightest sign of reciprocity, the attraction quickly fades. It isn't meant to be real.

## 10. ten

**It is not uncommon** for teenagers to have crushes like this for several months — or even years. Their day-to-day lives involve hanging out with their friends, trying to perfect the "art" of flirting, trying to concentrate on their studies (which requires some effort as their minds are elsewhere), and clashing with other family members because they feel misunderstood in their rebellious attitudes. Now they lock themselves in their rooms in their free time, put on music that evokes romantic feelings and imagine themselves living out the romance in all its plenitude, as if it were all real — or could easily come to be so. They imagine themselves with the person, strolling through fields or along a beach at sunset, whispering the words of love they have learned in books or romantic films. They construct entire narratives, kiss passionately and exchange promises of eternal love. These daydreams are essentially about tenderness and rarely involve any eroticism. Sex doesn't seem to fit the scenario!

When they awake from these daydreams, they feel a little sad because they aren't real. And they get very upset if they hear that their beloved is interested in some-

one else. But it isn't enough to make them give up on them, much less their fantasies; as soon as they can, they run through same enchanting daydream once again. They do it in moments of calm, alone at night, when they aren't busy with anything else. **At the age of 8 or 9, these were the hours when they felt the pain of forsakenness and tried to find ways to be close to their mothers. Now, instead of crying for their mothers, they have dream-romances with the person who is their "adult" substitute for the mother figure. The imagination provides a solution, albeit precarious, for a problem that didn't have one, such that at 15 they no longer need to cry for real cosiness. Substituting the mother with an "adult" object makes this obvious repetition seem more mature.**

This romantic fusion can only be experienced via the imagination, because if it were real it would be too much of a threat to their individuality. This fact contains an essential truth. It is actually very difficult to reconcile romantic fusion with a life that is not full of concessions. To willingly spend every waking moment with our loved one, we would have to always want to be in the same place at the same time. As I have said before, I think it is impossible. **In a nutshell, the fear that love might become something real is legitimate because it is a real threat to other desires that are just as or even more important. Those who hope to find a happy ending in love need to find a solid and consistent solution to this dilemma.**

Another phantom also lurks around the issue of sentimental ties: the fear of an unexpected and undesired separation (this is, of course, when the ties are real, since the risk doesn't exist when they are only imaginary). Even without any "adult"[9] experience in love we already know perfectly well how much break-ups can hurt. We all have some record of birth, our first and most dramatic separation. Throughout childhood, we experience temporary separations when our parents travel or get divorced, while the death of loved ones (such as grandparents) is permanent.

We know that the pain of sentimental separation is one of the worst kinds we can experience in life. We also know that they are not completely improbable, because every relationship is the embryo of a separation! In other words, it takes great courage to establish bonds.

In this particular aspect, in adolescence people start dividing into two large groups: those who don't deal well with frustration and obstacles and those who are better able to tolerate such things. Those who fall into the first category — who kick up a stink when things don't go the way they want them to — are unlikely to have the courage to truly become romantically involved. They generally learn to use the romantic vocabulary well and can give others the impression that they are

---

[9] I use quotation marks a lot because such obvious repetitions of childhood experiences in our adult lives deserve a special name.

really taking risks; but in reality they only get sentimentally involved in rather oblique ways, which I will describe a little further along.

Those who are better able to deal with suffering tend to be more daring and at some stage will try to find a real solution to the love-versus-individuality dilemma. They accept the risk of maybe having to deal with the pain of separation. Teenagers, who tend to feel omnipotent, often minimize and underestimate such risks because they don't believe bad things will happen to them, which certainly reinforces their courage to take the plunge in love.

# 11

eleven

**Sexuality manifests** at different moments throughout childhood, almost always in a less important manner. There are exceptions related to traumatic experiences that aren't the topic of this discussion, and there are also cases in which it is much more exuberantly expressed than usual, attracting the attention of other children and adults. With the exception of these cases, manifestations of sexuality are always essentially autoerotic: growing exhibitionist pleasure starting at around 6 or 7, and the manipulation of erogenous zones. When children exchange caresses, it is as if they were imitating adult behaviour. The exchange provokes arousal, because the sensitive regions receive the necessary tactile stimulus. But the partners are totally irrelevant, of the same or the opposite sex. They don't matter!

The exchange of caresses provokes sexual arousal, but this shouldn't be confused with lust. **Lust is different to arousal and manifests clearly in puberty. Arousal is "internal", while lust is "external", a desire to hold and possess. Lust implies an object — or objects. Arousal is indifferent to objects and can occur on its own. The object of lust can be relevant or not. In this**

**sense, lust is very different to love, in which the interest is specific and unique. Love is monogamous, while lust is, as a rule, promiscuous.**

With the appearance of adult sexuality, the arousal of visually stimulated lust surprises boys, who have previously been ambivalent about women. This brings on a great deal of masturbatory activity. Girls realize that they are attractive to men and also identify the ones they find more interesting.[10]

The first adult exchanges of caresses take place with partners chosen more selectively. Physical appearances become very relevant, along with other aspects of adolescent behaviour. These rather shy moments of physical intimacy are a more or less recent phenomenon. In the past, girls were not allowed to have any physical contact before they were officially "an item", while boys sought sexual initiation in brothels, or, if they were from the upper classes, with lower class girls. **Nowadays, teenagers' first erotic encounters take place between boys and girls of the same age group and socio-cultural background, which is a great step forward. They exchange limited erotic caresses in public places where everyone else is doing the same thing, and also, where everyone can see and be seen.**

Teenagers get with classmates and other teenagers at parties. They know little about one another, and

---

**10** There is debate as to whether women's desire is really tripped by visual stimuli. Personally, I don't think it is the case with most women.

the objective appears to be learning to deal with their own sexuality, as well as developing competence in their seductive abilities. The more daring are more successful. The more extroverted, good-looking, "popular" ones have countless partners between the ages of 13 to 18. The shyer, more guarded ones; the girls who think they are less attractive and the boys who are seen as lacking the attributes valued by the group are left out. They feel inferior and less competent in these first attempts in the game of seduction — which, over the years, tends to become more active and aggressive.

**It is interesting to note that the ones who are successful in erotic matters are not usually the most gifted or of the best character. Boys who are more forward, like girls who are exhibitionists, are generally selfish types. Their success in such matters provokes envy in their more serious, generous[11] peers. The ones who do well in school and show exemplary behaviour are not the ones who attract great erotic interest early on.**

Little by little, the fear of physical intimacy, especially strong in girls, starts to fade. Boys and girls get with each other, but the next day it is as if nothing of relevance has happened. There is generally no deepening of this physical intimacy, much less intellectual (especially in early adolescence). **Getting with one another doesn't go**

---

[11] I discuss my theory of the generous, the selfish, and the fair in-depth in my book *Evil, Good and Beyond*.

**Flávio Gikovate**

anywhere; it stays right where it is! Any continuity would imply an enormous risk of real romantic involvement, and we already know that this is cause for terror at the beginning of adult life, in which the best place for love is still the realm of fantasy.

## twelve

**When, finally,** at around 15 or 16 years of age, teenagers begin to pluck up the courage for real-life romantic involvement, curious and somewhat unexpected phenomena appear. I mentioned earlier that at the age of about 5 or 6 children start to choose their friends, namely those with whom they get along better because they are like-minded or because they laugh at the same things. During puberty and adolescence, friends become fundamentally important and are chosen according to the same criteria, intensified by their increasingly differentiated behaviour.

**Well, what do you know — our first boyfriends and girlfriends are not chosen from our groups of friends! On the contrary: if you ask a teenager why they don't go out with this or that special friend, they say that they're "not my type." It is obvious to me that they are exactly their type. But they say they aren't because they are not physically attracted to one another.**

If we consider that there are two basic types of human beings — those who tend to be more generous than selfish (who give more than they receive) and those who tend to be more selfish than generous (who take more than they give) — and that they are all more or less set in their ways, we would thus expect 50% of couples to be very similar in their behaviour (25% selfish-selfish pairings and 25% generous-generous) and 50% to be opposites. But this isn't what happens; in practice, more than 90% of relationships are between opposites and a few are between selfish individuals (who are always fighting and mistrustful of one another). There are hardly any relationships between generous sorts, except by sheer fluke! (The interesting thing is that this kind of relationship tends to develop very nicely.)

**There are many reasons why romantic involvements take this path. The only one that can't be used to explain this phenomenon is Cupid's poor archery.** Relationships between opposites occur with such regularity that they require explanations that consider more than mere chance. There are very strong reasons why people with great affinities are not emotionally attracted to one another.

**The first and most traditional has to do with cultural pressure, based on the idea that the ideal relationship is complementary, that is, between opposites** (this discourse has started to change, albeit slowly, over the last twenty years). **Young people are familiar with relationships between opposites at home and in the homes of relatives and friends.** Their parents are almost always opposites: one is more "explosive" (we say they have a "short fuse" or a "strong personality"), intolerant, aggressive, and selfish; while the other is tolerant, patient, docile, and more generous. Because they are like this and apparently love one another, this relationship model obviously influences the way their children think and behave.

**Additionally, it sounds like a good idea to have a partner who possesses the qualities that we don't (and vice-versa). The more aggressive one will make up for the more docile one's lack of courage, while the latter will make up for the former's lack of diplomacy. The generous one likes to give, while the selfish one needs to receive, giving the impression that they fit together perfectly, one concave and the other convex.** Unfortunately, this isn't the truth, since certain emotions, especially their reciprocal envy (inevitable between opposites who are in close contact), get in the way. Love is born of admiration. So is envy!

The cultural norm that encourages couplings between opposites was established in times past, when the main motivation was survival. The idea of being complementary to one another made sense, because such couples were better equipped to face their adverse habitats. But life has changed a lot and, with it, our motivations. Today, couples get together above all to enjoy life and one another's company, and their goals in life have more to do with leisure. Differences can be highly irritating and affinities have become much more important. Traditional beliefs need to be revisited and replaced with ideas more consistent with our new circumstances.

# 13
### thirteen

**Teenagers with good** self-esteem are rare. Self-esteem, as we know, isn't love for oneself; rather, it is self-judgment, the rating we give ourselves. The items assessed are typical of each phase of life, and for teenagers, physical appearances and popularity carry the most weight. Sporting prowess also ranks highly, as does success with the opposite sex. So-called character virtues are not terribly important, neither is discipline, and in some cases dedication to one's studies can even carry negative points. Intelligence is more or less important, but it is lower on the scale than sense of humour and the ability to entertain.

Adolescence is thus a phase that favours more extroverted sorts and those who are good at self-advertisement. Show-offs, who are bolder when it comes to flirting with the opposite sex, and girls who know how to get the boys' attention have a big advantage over shyer, more discreet, respectful types, who don't take initiatives for fear of rejection.

**Most selfish teenagers fall into the first group (the popular kids), while the generous ones fall into the second. The former generally find that things go**

**smoothly for them, and in their first few years of adult life they often have a positive self-image.** This image is shaken when they experience their first setbacks, because they are unable to deal well with pain. They suffer a lot when rejected by someone they desire, when they aren't good at a certain sport, or when they aren't as attractive as they would like to be.

They always go to great lengths to show how comfortable they are in their own skin, but suffer inwardly when faced with obstacles, always unwilling to accept their limitations. They deal with failure by blaming other people, never accepting responsibility for their own mistakes. If their family isn't in a good position financially, they get angry with their parents, blame them for the things they don't have, and demand things they have no right to. They are hotheaded at home but pose as happy when they are around their friends. They don't know how to be alone and have little patience for individual activities — reading, studies, research on the computer, etc. As the years go by, they clearly recognize their limitations.

Shyer teenagers have no doubt that they are the losers, because they don't have the right social skills, and don't consider themselves good-looking, much less sexually attractive. They are discreet and lead more reserved lives; they spend more time at home and have only a handful of good friends (who are in a similar situation to themselves). They don't make any effort to pose as winners, because they don't believe in their ability to pull it off. When they are intellectually gifted and disciplined, they devote themselves to their studies and try to seek distinction in this area, although they know that this kind of success is not held in very high esteem by their peers. But it is what is within their reach.

They have big hopes for the future, dream of successful careers and believe that this is how they might one day be able to reverse their unfavourable situation. They tend to be persistent, determined, and more tolerant of setbacks. They are docile, dreamers, and romantics (in part because they don't see themselves as competent players in the game of seduction). They accept a bad present in favour of a better future reasonably well, contrary to more selfish sorts, who generally want everything in the here and now.

None of them are happy with themselves. The selfish, when very good-looking, might actually feel better about themselves than most teenagers; in these cases, they may be attracted to other selfish sorts who feel just as good about themselves. They build tense relationships full of jealousy, which gives rise to terrible fights that quickly erode the relationship. The generous are definitely not happy with themselves due to their limited social success. They rarely enter relationships with other generous sorts unless circumstances push them to, such as when they are the only two left in a particular group — who, for lack of other options, get together.

The overwhelming majority of boys and girls are fascinated by their opposites, because admiration and pragmatism are the driving forces behind attraction. If they are not satisfied with and proud of themselves, they will try to be around people with the qualities they would like to have. The generous seek extroverted, bold partners. The selfish seek reliable, persistent sorts, with whom they feel safer. It is of the essence of the selfish to desire (or need) to feel loved in a way that makes them feel safe. This is easier with generous partners, even if they don't inspire their admiration. Selfish sorts are more pragmatic, while generous sorts are more romantic.

**The reasons outlined** in the previous chapter have a big influence on the fact that first relationships usually take place between opposites. There are also other motives, perhaps even more relevant. One of them is the fear of love — the same fear that leads teenagers to only have fantasy crushes in their early adolescence. **It eventually fades enough to allow them to have real involvements, but it doesn't disappear.** This means the relationship can't be too intense. Full sentimental involvement would be an enormous threat to their individuality — which is still forming during their youth.

**The fear of love arises whenever one's individuality is at risk. In this phase of life, people feel less threatened, but not enough to be able to deal with real sentimental intensity. The selfish are more afraid of involvement, because they don't believe they are strong enough to deal with the pain of a break-up, if it were to happen. As a result, they assume a curious stance, quite in keeping with their personality type: they accept being the object of love more than actually loving.** They want the benefits of being loved by someone. They want to be the "muse" (man or woman) who receives the attention and beautiful words of the "poet".

#### Flávio Gikovate

The generous appear to have more courage to surrender to the emotion of love, since they are better able to deal with suffering and thus don't run from the risk of separation inherent in any relationship. Additionally, they are much better at giving than receiving, which makes them feel superior and proud. They suffer from low self-esteem, especially when young, and are fascinated by the extroversion and social success of the selfish. It is easy to understand how they are attracted to them and make them the object of their love. The selfish are comfortable receiving, which is completely in keeping with their aspirations. They give very little, which is even better!

**The generous love and are dedicated. The selfish are loved and take what they are given. It seems like a good arrangement: they each have everything the other doesn't — not to mention the fact that this type of relationship goes hand in hand with our cultural beliefs.** We feel as if we were just half of something when alone, and complete when we "meld" with our other half. Complementary fusion is thus convenient for everyone.

**Let's reflect a little more on the courage to love of the generous. Truth be told, they love without being loved! They love people who are happy to take but don't give back in the same proportion. Sometimes I think this is closer to the fantasy love of adolescence than a real relationship. Everything happens as if the generous were dreaming a love story that wasn't really happening. It is experienced unilaterally, because the selfish are in the relationship to reap its benefits.** Their circumstances are completely different. The generous live out a love story, while the selfish are happy to receive and are not terribly concerned about being loyal, dedicated, or even sincere. They are always demanding more attention and often show signs of jealousy — falsely interpreted as proof of their love, when in reality it indicates their fear of losing their benefits. Their romantic discourse may be similar, but their behaviour and experience of things are incredibly different.

**If this is true, then the generous also lack the courage for the romantic fusion for which they supposedly yearn.** They complain of the disregard and rude behaviour of the selfish — but if they weren't like this, the generous probably wouldn't be attracted to them. They claim to want fusion and lament that they don't have it because of the limitations of their selfish partners, but they won't change their generous conduct (which reinforces their partner's selfishness) for anything in the world. They dream of whole love and live half relationships: the qualities of the selfish incite attraction and fascination, while their limitations and flaws create a distancing that impedes plenitude. They may behave like they are frustrated, but this is typically cunning. They consider themselves to be ready for love and transfer the whole problem — including their own emotional limitations — onto their partner.[12]

---

**12** My reflections on this subject have made me increasingly sceptical about the moral fibre and consistency of generosity.

fifteen

**As if the reasons** set forth in previous chapters were not enough, there is another very important one that propels people to seek partners who are their opposites. It is sexual desire. The generous feel a strong attraction to the selfish, but I don't believe the opposite is true. In other words, the selfish are also attracted to the selfish! This explains why, as I mentioned previously, there are relationships between selfish partners (which are very successful from an erotic point of view) early in adult live. The generous don't feel sexually attracted to people who are like themselves, nor are the selfish drawn to them. This is an extremely complex issue that requires much more clarification, but which I won't go into here. However, because the generous are more likely to get romantically involved, the initiative, in spite of everything, will come from them. **They are only attracted to more selfish sorts: nice boys are drawn to girls who are exhibitionists (even slightly vulgar), while nice girls are fascinated by "bad boys".**

The selfish — perhaps after a painful experience with a partner similar to themselves — eventually realize that other selfish people are not very trustworthy and start to accept romantic overtures from the generous, even if their sex appeal isn't as strong. They enjoy being their partners' object of desire and love. They puff up with vanity, which is a kind of erotic pleasure. They also feel much more secure and believe they hold great power over their partners — which, for them, is always good.

It is intriguing to see that sex appeal closely resembles the behaviour of the selfish. We cannot, therefore, underestimate how much it might reinforce selfish behaviour. What do they have that makes them so attractive? Is it their apparent brazenness and exhibitionism? It may be part of it, but I think there's still more to it. Because the selfish have more relaxed morals, those around them feel less concerned about being judged according to a code of values. Although the selfish are always making demands and complaining, they actually aren't critical of others' behaviour; they only criticise those who don't do what they want them to!

The selfish want everything in the here and now and live for the present. They are — or appear to be — more like crickets than ants.[13] This receptivity to all things pleasurable suggests to others that they are very competent in erotic matters, freer of norms and prejudices. While they aren't really like this in real life, they do manage to pass themselves off as such.

Because they are more extroverted and self-centred, they appear to be more independent and individualistic,

---

**13** A reference to French poet Jean de La Fontaine's *The Ant and the Cricket.*

which also seems to be part of their sex appeal. They give others the impression that they don't get emotionally involved and won't require any kind of romantic continuity — which alleviates others' fear of love and loosens up their sensuality.

These are just some considerations about a phenomenon I have been trying to understand better for decades. I believe the mysteries of sex are harder to unravel than the mysteries of love — which I hope to decode in the course of this book.

# 16
### sixteen

**Our first stable,** long-term relationships thus tend to take place between a more generous person and a more selfish person. Gender doesn't have an influence, such that the generous one might be the man or the woman and vice-versa. On a scale of 0 to 10, the generous one gives, say, 10 and receives 5. The selfish one receives 10 and gives 5. Everything appears to fit together very nicely and, for a time, the relationship goes well, since both are receiving within their expectations. There are degrees of giving and taking and there can be relationships in which the generous one gives 10 and receives 1 and the selfish one gives 1 and receives 10. As a rule, people who are selfish and generous in the same "proportion" tend to have more stable relationships, and we can infer a lot about a person from the partner he or she has chosen. Something like: **"Tell me who you love, and I'll tell you who you are!"**

When the distance from the point of equilibrium is small, that is, in a relationship between someone who is "slightly selfish" and someone who is "slightly generous", there can be real, lasting stability. The selfish one is easy to spot: he or she is always the one that complains the most. Slightly selfish people don't complain a lot and, as a rule, are satisfied with what they receive. They are a little more explosive, but their intolerance of obstacles isn't radical. They are reasonably at ease in their own skin and don't think they are much worse than their partners, since, in their own way, they are also dedicated to them. The same thing is valid for those who are slightly generous, satisfied with the dimension of the imbalance, which not only doesn't importune them, but also feeds their vanity. They are generous, but are fairly competent at standing up for their rights and their main demands are met.

The problems are much bigger when both are further from the point of equilibrium — which, unfortunately, is more common. Hostile manifestations of envy appear more forcefully. We envy that which we value but do not have. The selfish envy the sweet, tolerant, giving nature of the generous. At the same time that they benefit from their dedication and always want more, they feel humiliated and belittled; they need to receive but, deep down, would really like to be self-sufficient.

**Envy is an aggressive reaction sparked by an action also understood as aggressive, although invisible in an initial analysis. After all, the generous position themselves as those who "only want to help". At least that is the official story.** In reality, the generous know very well that, by giving, they are placing themselves in a position of superiority and humiliating their partner. Proof of this is in the way they react when they receive:

they hate the situation and feel awkward and humiliated. In giving too much they know they are inflicting pain on the selfish — who can't refuse the offering because they need it.

What kind of impulse drives this aggressive manifestation on the part of the generous — using dedication as a weapon? Envy, once again. It may seem like a paradox to those who consider generosity a virtue, a much higher state than selfishness, which is treated as a serious flaw.[14] The truth is, the generous envy the selfish for their capacity to enjoy material life to its fullest and to grant themselves so many rights, the way they want everything here and now, and their apparently laid-back approach to life and the future. They envy above all the sensual power of the selfish and the ease with which they circulate socially.

The generous aren't capable of head-on confrontations. They don't know how to do it, just as they don't know how to say "no" even when they want to. They are reined in by feelings of guilt. They feel guilty even when they are not actually responsible for whatever the selfish are complaining about. The selfish impose their will and attack head-on because they are unable to control their impulses, especially aggressive ones. The generous humiliate them more by being increasingly generous, motivated by the erroneous idea that they will one day manage to seduce and "domesticate" the

---

[14] This isn't my point of view, which I explain in detail in *Bad, Good and Beyond*.

selfish. In fact, their growing generosity has an aggressive, rancorous objective — to progressively humiliate and weaken the person who attacks them. **One partner attacks head-on, the other, subtly and by being nice, thus circumventing their fears and feelings of guilt.**

The relationship is, therefore, essentially violent, and with the passing years the differences grow more radical. There is great interdependence because each one takes advantage of the other's attributes. The generous enjoy the ability of the selfish to be aggressive and demand things in the here and now; while the selfish enjoy their partners' tolerance and dedication. This kind of relationship usually lasts long enough to lead to marriage, thus forming a "diabolical alliance" in which everyone loses. It is not a relationship in which both partners can grow, since great emotional advances don't happen. They just become more and more set in their ways as time goes by.

# 17
seventeen

**In relationships** in which the selfish partner is the man, things tend to be calmer and more stable than when it is the woman. This is due, above all, to sexist cultural norms (still in a process of transformation), which grant men certain privileges. This imbalance in favour of men originally had to do with the fact that men had to be providers, among other reasons. But even when they are no longer the sole breadwinners, they still retain certain benefits. For example, in many cases they can arrive home later without it being treated as a serious offence; although the opposite is not true.

More selfish men go to bars for drinks with their friends after work, play sports on the weekends even when their wives are at home busy with housework and looking after the kids. They wouldn't, however, accept the same from their wives. These men are jealous and could never swallow the limitations they impose on their partners. They use the fact that they still bring home the largest portion of the family income to justify dubious privileges. Their generous wives (who give more than they receive), are usually fine with these unfair differences. They like this self-denial in favour of their husbands because it allows them to exercise their generosity.

More selfish sorts tend to be more envious. In this particular situation, the men are rarely envious of their wives, because they compensate their admiration for their wives' dedication to their family with the fact that they feel professionally and financially superior. An important ingredient that gives rise to pointless arguments is thus not as present in these relationships. More generous women tend to be less envious and competitive and rebel less against the arbitrariness of their situation.

Every now and then these husbands are caught lying and cheating, whether in situations involving indiscretions with other women or those related to work, money, and friends, etc. People who don't deal well with frustration and obstacles are less reliable because they are unable to "tame" all of their desires and impulses, since any renouncement generates frustration. **They are not always able to control strong sexual impulses. Because they can't keep a lid on their aggression, they get into traffic brawls and unnecessary conflicts at work and can do themselves considerable damage in this area — and they don't always tell their wives about these things.**

The husband's unreliability can be the undoing of this kind of relationship. The wives, tolerant and docile, may slowly start to lose their admiration for their husbands. For many, it is as if they have gone too far and taken their dedication for granted. Things can sometimes take a while to get to this point precisely because

the wives tend to pardon everything. But the endless lies, rude behaviour when they don't get what they want at home, and explosions (where they get very offensive for a few minutes and then act as if nothing ever happened) start to undermine their wives' goodwill. Bad experiences are not easily forgotten.

**The wives' loss of admiration for their gregarious, virile husbands, whom they used to consider good sexual partners, usually manifests precisely in this area. Previously sexually giving, these generous wives gradually lose the desire for sexual intimacy. It's as if they're saying their first, radical NO to their husbands. This rebellion doesn't manifest in words, but through the body: orgasms become rare and their interest in sex dwindles.**

These marriages are apparently harmonious, but in reality they are ruled by weakness, where the men have a low frustration tolerance ("explosive tempers") and get worked up easily over very little and the women's feelings of guilt stop them from standing up for their legitimate rights. The harmony is broken when, tired of the humiliations they have tolerated until now, the wives start to show signs of dissatisfaction. They first raise their heads in the area of sex, putting an end to what had previously been a very successful erotic partnership.

## eighteen

**Couples in which** the generous partner is the man have a peculiar problematic, different to the one described in the previous chapter. In these cases, the woman is usually particularly attractive, at least in his eyes. More selfish women know that much of their partners' fascination is derived from this fact, and they take great care with their appearances. Their behaviour is usually somewhat provocative and exhibitionist. Selfish women are usually sociable and love to be desired by all men. This reinforces the usual insecurities and jealousy in their partners. The men usually feel proud to be with such a coveted, attractive woman. They consider themselves privileged — as well as jealous.

A selfish woman requires a lot of attention and always demands more and more. **Her generous husband will go out of his way to cater to her whims, be they material or regarding his presence and the way he acts towards her. He hopes she will one day praise him, telling him she is proud of him and completely satisfied with his behaviour.** On this day, she will let down her armour and show him that she loves him as much as he

**Flávio Gikovate**

loves her. He will be fully corresponded in his feelings. He lives for this day, which usually never comes.

Selfish men have it much easier than generous men (even when they are married to equally as selfish women), because they spend less time at home and have lots of friends. They pay less attention to their wives, who tend not to stand up for themselves as much. Generous men, on the other hand, tend to go from home to work and back again. They work a lot because they like it, but also because they believe that it will increase their chances of being admired and valued by their wives. When they are late arriving home they are greeted with scowls and raised voices, when they were hoping for comprehension and pampering as if they had just come home from "battle". They dream of the day their home will be a "warrior's haven". They yearn for kind words and get the opposite.

**A selfish woman is more of an exhibitionist. As a rule, she is also jealous — even though she is married to a more reliable man. She believes that men are very susceptible to women's sensual power, which is true: after all, she knows that this was one of the main reasons why he chose her. She considers her husband to be somewhat naive, and vulnerable to the erotic manipulation of other women — much like her own behaviour. She fears that her man is easy prey for other unscrupulous women. In this aspect, she guards him like a treasure. In private, however, the opposite is true: she treats him as if he were highly uninteresting,** while

he bends over backwards to prove himself better and more able, more dedicated to pleasing her in order to erase the negative image she pretends to have of him.

The generous husband arrives home full of romantic fantasies. It's as if he's forgotten that yesterday she wasn't speaking to him. Maybe today will be different (after all, the selfish are unpredictable) and he will be well received. Maybe today he'll get lucky and have that night of lovemaking he so longs for but which rarely happens (selfish women love to provoke but are rarely giving in bed). She makes him desire her, but isn't interested in the act itself, making him feel frustrated, humiliated, and rejected. He thinks this can change if he has an even more positive attitude, and is more loving, more competent, more successful. The harder he tries, the less successful he is. **His sex life is one continuous frustration. She knows this and grows even more concerned that another woman might try to win him over; and her jealousy grows. The contradictions are enormous and intrigue the generous husband, who doesn't know how to decipher all these signals.**

She almost always rejects him sexually (only throwing him the occasional crumb), although she is terrified some floozy might come along and give him what he longs for. She treats him as if he isn't worth much, but doesn't want to lose him at any cost. She threatens to leave him whenever she thinks it's necessary. He quakes in his boots and she is thus reassured that the idea isn't in his plans. But one day he gets tired of it all

and suggests they part ways. She grovels and begs him to reconsider. She behaves better for a few days and then everything goes back to "normal".

He loves and admires her for her apparent boldness and, above all, for her physical and sensual attributes. She admires him for the determination, persistence, and discipline that she doesn't have. She admires his generosity and capacity for love. She admires and envies him. **Envy, in this case, is the key to understanding almost everything: she tries to destroy his self-esteem — especially as regards his virility — so he won't escape her. She acts aggressively because of the anger and desire for retaliation that this envy awakens in her.**

One day he realizes that his dedication only causes her envy to grow. Feeling stronger, he begins a process of inversion, trying to reposition himself and her in more appropriate roles. If unsuccessful in this endeavour, he might decide to embark on other romantic possibilities — to her distaste and despair.

**More selfish people** tend to repeat the same patterns over and over. It makes sense, because their intention is to continue reaping benefits in a relationship in which they have the upper hand. When a selfish man's relationship ends, he will look for a new generous partner, who, for a time, will be dedicated to him. She may eventually tire of the relationship and decide to break it off. He will look for younger and younger partners, perhaps more naïve and inexperienced, as well as more physically attractive. They are easily drawn in by the self-promotional discourse in which he is a master.

A selfish woman will also look for another generous partner. They are more docile, loyal and, at least for a while, easily manipulated. The sexual problem will tend to repeat itself: diminished sex drive and inability to share herself with a generous man, whom she admires and envies. She isn't terribly loyal, so if her sexual needs are intense she will find a way to satisfy them with a lover who is a little more selfish than she is. She will play the role of the generous one in this parallel relationship (which is only possible while she is in the first), and in this condition will be

sexually willing in a way that is totally impossible with her generous partner. This is because here there is no **envy to inhibit her desire to please.**

I sometimes have a hard time understanding why generous men and women tend to repeat inadequate choices. They have already suffered so much in the past and still act as if they have learned nothing! They remain sexually fascinated by untrustworthy show-offs and keep making their choices accordingly. A generous woman will still have a good sex partner in a selfish man. But what about the generous man, eternally humiliated and rejected? Why would he get involved with the same kind of woman again?

I think we need to look for other motivations beyond the undeniable erotic fascination that the selfish inspire in the generous — and everyone else. We should never be content with a single explanation for any given behaviour. Most of our behaviour patterns are underpinned by multiple causes. I think the apparent naivety of the hypothesis that the new partner might eventually change and the relationship become richer actually masks an emotional immaturity that makes the generous want to be loved without being loved back. The generous want to be brimming with love and live with the dream of having a good partner, whom they have chosen exactly for who they are. **In other words, generous people who are fascinated by the selfish are at a stage of development in which this is exactly what they want; they aren't as naïve as they appear to be. They** aren't ready for anything more than this in terms of emotional intimacy.

Another reason has to do with vanity. Those who give more than they receive are validated by the code of ethics of our culture and may feel superior to those receiving their favours. They like to feel good, strong, rich, and selfless, able to give up everything they have to please or benefit their loved ones — as well as other people. Self-sacrifice makes them feel heroic, which pleases them immensely. It masks the fear of rejection and guilty feelings that cause the generous to tilt the scales in favour of others and to make their weaknesses a kind of strength. Those who give somehow sense that their generosity humiliates those on the receiving end, making them feel ill at ease; in this "honourable" way, they thus avenge themselves of the hostilities of the selfish.

In addition to boosting their inner pride, derived from their ability to relinquish so much and give the other person what they want so badly (and can't get on their own), they close the doors on any retribution, which causes the beneficiary great discomfort. It reinforces the selfish partner's dependence and eases any insecurities and fear of abandonment the generous partner might feel. Weakening their partner is part of their strategy for controlling them — even though superficially the generous one appears totally dominated and manipulated by the selfish partner.

The power games between them are no laughing matter. If I am correct in my assessment, it is impossible

not to see generosity as a form of moral violence every bit as atrocious as selfishness. A dynamic is established between them in which cruelty reins, explicit or disguised. This is not the terrain of emotional happiness.

**Nowadays** it is less and less common for relationships between opposites to last "until death do us part". (In the past this was the rule, because the idea of complementary partners was valued and those who parted ways were punished with social rejection.) Break-ups, generally instigated by the generous, take place at some stage while a couple is courting, engaged, or married. The selfish only usually take the initiative to end relationships when they are very young, at a stage when they think they are superior to their partners and can find better ones. Some end relationships because they are seduced by the temptations of single life, for which they really are well suited. They rarely do so after having established a stronger practical dependence.

**The generous take the initiative to break up marriages in three circumstances: when life together has become unbearable; when they become emotionally involved with someone else; or in the rare cases in which they feel ready to be on their own — even when life in common isn't such a disaster.** In all cases they suffer a lot, since separation always recalls our first separation — birth.

# A Love Story...
**Flávio Gikovate**

Even when he has another relationship in sight, a generous man getting a divorce (obviously everything is much easier when the couple isn't married) feels bad for not being present in the home and his children's daily lives. The situation is even worse when he decides to live alone, because he is not cut out for typical single life: he is not accustomed to going out and having superficial contact with a lot of people, much less casual sexual encounters without continuity. As well as not feeling comfortable in these activities, he usually isn't very successful, since the selfish tend to outshine him in this area.

**Partners who take the initiative to break up generally suffer less, at least initially. They miss the cosiness and may feel helpless and lost. But they won't experience the pain of rejection that is so offensive to one's vanity, nor will they feel supplanted.** This is a terrible pain for anyone, especially the selfish, who deal very badly with setbacks and frustrations. They try to avoid the pain — as well as the public humiliation of being dumped — and resort to all manner of threats, involving aggression towards others and themselves. They act with violence or use emotional blackmail. It is at these times that they really expose their weaknesses and show their true colours.

**If the generous partner is not strong and resolute, he or she will give in to the pressure, out of guilt and pity. Which is why the generous only tend to end relationships when they are already interested in someone else; their feelings for the other person end up tilting**

the scales in favour of separation. They rarely have the determination and self-esteem to stand up to all the pressure with the objective of being on their own. In both cases, the generous person will have to be single for a while and face long hours of solitude in contexts in which he or she has little experience. Few men know how to stay home alone. Women are much better at this, and it isn't so rare for them to initiate a break-up with the intention of being alone. They also prefer solitude because unpleasant married life is worse for them; men who are frustrated in their relationships often pour themselves into their work.

There is another factor that favours women: in marriage break-ups, it is more common for them to get the house and kids. Even more generous women don't give up these rights so easily. They only do so in extreme situations, which I won't go into here. Generous men are more likely to grant a larger portion of the assets to their selfish wives, as well as the home and custody of the children. They believe they lose certain rights for having taken the initiative to separate and, once again, accept an uneven division — so typical of their personality type! Generous women give up more, but not the home or their children, and thus suffer a little less, especially in the beginning.

# 21
twenty one

**Both the generous** and the selfish suddenly find themselves alone. It is unexpected because even today people think of marriage as something solid and resistant to wear and tear. The shock is greatest in marriages where there are children. But even when shorter relationships and marriages (without children) break up, the suffering is great. Intellectually we know that loving relationships are transitory, but we live them as if they were eternal. The break-up, even when wanted, is another big bang. As I have said before, the pain of those who have been rejected is terrible. The separation brings back feelings of forsakenness.

A strange feeling related to the loss of certain habits, routines, and even tension and strife, is normal in the early days of being alone. People feel as if a "hole" has appeared in their stomachs (actually, it reappears, as it has been attenuated until now by the emotional connection). Feelings of forsakenness and rejection are hard to deal with, even for those with a high pain threshold. These initial moments — a kind of mourning for a connection intended to be eternal — are experienced as loneliness.

This very strong pain is only felt during the transition that occurs when one member of a relationship pulls away and goes back to being a single person. It is not a permanent, irremediable state of mind typical of those who are alone. Strong pain is felt in transitions experienced as negative, while pleasures are characteristic of positive transitions. Pleasure and pain are always finite, because we later get used to our new condition, positive or negative.

A better word for the state following this transition is, perhaps, solitude, which involves getting used to life as a single person. It should not be confused with the traumatic period related to grieving and loss of references due to broken routines. Some people claim that solitude can be very nice!

People who are frightened by the first phase of being alone scramble to find new romantic relationships. They are in a terrible way emotionally, and their urgency makes them less picky about whom they get involved with. Because they don't choose carefully they will suffer frustration and disappointment in the new relationship, and once again they will experience the pain related to separation. By trying to rid themselves of this kind of suffering, they find themselves facing it once again.

If they are not careful and do not deal with the pain they are trying to avoid, they will make the same mistake over and over, and their criteria for choosing partners is unlikely to change. The process does not lead to growth and is a vicious circle. It is like a car bogged in

mud; when someone steps on the accelerator, it only makes the problem worse. Their self-esteem is shaken by successive failures, which creates almost imperative conditions for the pattern to remain unbroken. People need to stop and think a lot before they act. They need to be prudent and look for a legitimate way out of their rut, which means facing pain — rather than trying to escape it.

# 22
twenty two

**The possibility** of a new life starts to unveil itself when a person finishes grieving over a break-up. However long it lasts (we should always try to make it as short as possible), it is only afterwards that solitude — of the "useful", evolutionary, and constructive variety — begins. Solitude, as we know, is a chronic state that can last indefinitely and doesn't have to be bad. There are, of course, difficult moments. In the beginning, for example, we haven't the slightest idea how to dine out alone, nor are we accustomed to going to the movies or parties alone.

In many cultures, people feel bad when they are seen unaccompanied. It's as if there were a hierarchy that privileged married people or those in stable relationships. Fortunately, this is changing. It is interesting to note how strongly culture affects our subjectivity: if we are in a city — Paris or New York, for example — where it is normal for people to dine out alone, we are fine with it, and feel proud to do so. We see films, shop, and go sightseeing without a worry in the world, and make a mental note to adopt these new, attractive habits when we get back to our own country. But who are

### Flávio Gikovate

we kidding? After a few days we go straight back to all the local behaviours we had intended to abandon.

We sometimes have sensations typical of forsakenness — a "hole" in the stomach or a heavy feeling in the chest. Fear and insecurity assail us in everyday situations and we miss the comfort of a relationship. Little by little we "tame" these uncomfortable feelings: we realize that the symptoms disappear when we are busy, so we try to entertain ourselves as much as possible, working, reading, watching films, etc. We mostly feel uncomfortable when we are unoccupied, exactly like children who go to spend the weekend with friends and start missing their mothers at bedtime.

Nights can be more problematic, because it is when we feel particularly vulnerable. We may miss having another body beside us in bed, especially during winter. Slowly, however, we realize that this is a two-edged sword and that it is nice to be able to turn out the light whenever we want, to decide how many blankets to have on the bed without having to negotiate with a partner who has other preferences, or to choose what TV program we want to watch and when we want to watch it.

**The experience of being in charge of one's life starts to grow in importance. We decide if and what to eat, where to go, which invitations to accept, what to do. With time, this pleasure can outweigh the pain of forsakenness. In fact, the feeling of forsakenness is gradually replaced with one of wellbeing, born of self-sufficiency. It is a period of great emotional**

**growth and maturing: instead of being adults with childish needs, we start to find the strength to nurse our own "wounds" without the help of our mother — or her substitute.**

Important moral growth is always associated with this emotional growth in the direction of autonomy. The generous will now have to learn to do more for themselves, and the selfish will have to fend for themselves since they no longer have someone to lean on. The generous are incompetent at caring for themselves and will have to learn to do so. They know how to give to others but need to learn to give to themselves. The selfish are incompetent at caring for themselves and will have to learn to do so; they must learn to satisfy their own needs.

It is hard to imagine a situation more favourable to growth than this phase of life on one's own. It would be wonderful if, at some stage in their adult lives, everyone tried it, with the clear intention of trying to resolve the outstanding issues that we all bring with us from childhood.

twenty three

**Many people** in unhappy marriages, dissatisfied with the quality of their relationships, decide to carry on as they are. In most cases, the dissatisfied one is the more generous partner. When they become aware of their condition (that they love unilaterally and that the relationship is, above all, more convenient for the selfish partner) they realize what fools they have been. They no longer derive any pleasure in feeling stronger or "superior" because they give more than they receive.

When this happens, generous wives lose interest in their husbands sexually, while generous husbands stop indulging their wives and "begging" for their favours. Selfish men are usually very satisfied with their marriages, in spite of all their complaining; they are only disgruntled when they notice their wives' disinterest. Selfish women complain that they aren't interested sexually in their husbands, but think it's worth staying in the relationship, which offers many other conveniences. When selfish men and women realize that their partners are not pandering to their every-whim, they protest loudly — and their demands are met, albeit begrudgingly. The selfish calm down and go back to taking things for granted. They're quite happy for things to stay like this for the rest of their lives.

Even after the reality of their situation has sunk in, the generous tend to drag their feet. An exception to this rule is women who have no choice but to separate because of their husbands' violence. But when the husbands are "just" neglectful or womanizers, they lead their lives as if they were single. They look after themselves, their children, their homes, and spend a lot of time — previously the terrain of rejection and abandonment, but which they now treat as free time — reading, taking courses, catching up with their girlfriends, learning and devoting themselves to their own interests. By a different route, they also end up achieving the emotional and moral growth necessary for new possibilities to open up.

For both men and women, practical issues have a great influence on their decision to stay in a marriage. In the name of convenience, they tolerate the emptiness and frustration they feel as a result of being with a partner who disappoints them — from whom they no longer expect anything. Children count a lot, as do the family home, assets, and even the routine of married life. Beaten wives, however, often see no other option but separation, even when this implies serious practical obstacles.

Men, as I have said before, are less likely to want to separate. They are incompetent at being alone and pay a greater practical price for having to distance themselves from the children and the home, and may end up in a difficult financial situation — due to the duty to

maintain everything they have left behind. They are rarely so tormented that they can't continue as they are, fleeing the home with the pretext of working. They travel more than necessary and slowly begin to learn the art of being on their own. They learn to look after themselves, to make meals for one, and grant themselves growing benefits.

**More generous men and women stay in their marriages with partners who are their opposites, but become increasingly occupied with their own lives. They free themselves of the naïve hope of one day being treated with the consideration and respect they had hoped for as repayment for being so dedicated.** It becomes clear to them that they aren't going to grow old beside their partners, but they know that the sensible thing to do is accept their dubious situation until they are emotionally ready to spread their wings. When they have children, they think they have time. The children are growing up and, except in cases of extreme incompatibility, it is better for their development for their mother and father to stay together.

This process of maturing enough to be able to end the relationship usually takes a few years after they are fully aware of the irreversibility of their marital situation. This can be sped up by the appearance of an intense emotional involvement with another partner. If this happens before the necessary emotional growth has taken place, the new romantic involvement can be tense and have disastrous results.

# 24
twenty four

**The single life** of the selfish is quite different to that of the generous. The latter are more reserved, discreet, and shyer, and as such not well suited to superficial social contact. They are not the sorts who join clubs and know almost everyone after only a few weeks. They don't have the courage to approach people they don't know, because they are afraid of disturbing them or being rejected. They were not very successful socially when they were younger.

The generous tend to be homebodies and rarely go to singles events. When they do it is on the insistence of friends or family. They generally don't have a good time and chide themselves for having gone. They don't like the meat market atmosphere! They feel humiliated going to singles bars with the clear intention of finding a partner. It seems to offend their vanity because, among other reasons, they're no good at it — due to their temperament and because they don't feel comfortable in the role they are trying to play. They come out of these experiences with the clear feeling that they weren't cut out for this kind of lifestyle.

**The situation is even more awkward for men, because they see their bolder, more extroverted (gener-**

**ally selfish) friends in action. They are direct and frontal, and approach women who appear to be available — who are, as a rule, selfish. The selfish find sexual partners with incredible ease, and the generous feel humiliated and diminished by their incompetence.** They are not capable of overtly erotic overtures because they worry about offending women. They can't lie, and don't know how to be romantic when they are not interested in someone. They don't know what to do.

They feel like losers, stay at home more and more, hang out with their few friends, and hope to find a new partner in life's natural contexts: a party at a friend's place, at work, in the course of day-to-day life, etc. They get better at being alone and end up spending most of their time at work or in solitary pursuits of a cultural nature. When they play sports, they use the sporting environment to make friends. They feel much better going to places for an objective reason — and looking for a partner is not part of these activities.

**Generous women take a similar approach to single life, but I think they resent it a little less than generous men. They don't admire or envy the more uninhibited, extravagant women who are so successful at singles bars. They don't look for this kind of solution for their lives, they don't find the chase fun in itself, nor do they enjoy casual sexual intimacy. They want to find new steady partners. This being the objective, they are demanding and wait more or less patiently for them to appear.**

They hope to find someone better than those who have already passed through their lives, but it isn't easy and can take a long time to happen. The dangers they face — and this goes for men too — are desperation, the pain of being alone for so long, and giving up hope. I have already mentioned this situation, in which they may allow themselves to be approached by people who aren't right for them, repeating "choices" they had sworn not to make again. These regressive solutions can be irreversible. **I think it is better to leave the future open — even with no guarantee of success — than accept a warmed up "consolation prize".**

The selfish don't bother learning to be alone. They use their social skills to avoid any and all introspection. The minute they wake up they start to communicate with colleagues, acquaintances in general — all treated like friends. They chat on the phone and via instant messaging programs, work out at fashionable gyms, work, have lunch with the "gang", go for drinks after work, then to restaurants, and then out on the town. They always have several prospective sexual partners in sight. They are generally fairly successful in the game of seduction and have an active sex life. They have fun with selfish partners, but keep an eye out for someone more generous when the objective is establishing more lasting ties. They don't trust other selfish people, much less the "easy" types they meet at nightclubs. Because they are not good at being alone and are successful in their social lives, they tend to carry on like this even when they are already a little bored.

# A Love Story...
**Flávio Gikovate**

The selfish never show their boredom, always posing as happy and content with their deeds and achievements. They know that this provokes envy in the generous and they never miss an opportunity to pass themselves off as winners. And, in this aspect of single life, they really are! When they manage to emotionally seduce a new, more reliable partner, they relax, thanks to this new relationship. Because their capacity to tolerate frustration is low, they rarely give up the erotic pleasures of the single lives in which they were so successful. They try to have the best of both worlds. **In most cases they evolve little and just change partners. The courage to love doesn't develop in a lifestyle like the one I have just described, such that their emotional perspectives are rather bleak. Those who want to change their outlook will have to travel the most painful path — of honestly recognizing their difficulties and intolerances, and preparing to deal with them. They will have to try not to give in to the easy-come easy-go aspects of single life and find some alone time — so difficult and painful, but so rich in introspection and self-knowledge.**

# 25
twenty five

**We have come** to one of the most difficult moments in the journey of those who want to be happy in love and realize that they have the courage to try. The selfish usually lack this courage, because daring means risking failure, frustration, and running into obstacles. These moments are ripe for growth, and those who want quality relationships should not miss the opportunity, which may be one of their last chances to change the course of their lives.

Time passes painfully for generous types who are unhappily married — who lead solitary lives — as well as singles who are more reserved. Selfish people who are married are, as I explained earlier, generally satisfied with their state, in spite of all their grumbling. Those who are single, while perhaps a little bored, still manage to entertain themselves more easily with "friends", flings, and partying. They know they can't expect much in their emotional lives, regardless of their discourse: they seek relationships in which they have some kind of practical or emotional advantage, and nothing more.

The generous are bitter about the lack of sparkle in their lives. The married ones are disenchanted and tired of unilateral love. The single ones don't know where to

**Flávio Gikovate**

go, where to meet like-minded people. They stay at home, sad, but at peace with themselves. They feel like fish out of water at bars and parties. They lament that it is hard to find loyal friends and, more importantly, emotional partners, and complain of the scarcity of interesting people who want committed relationships. The idea of picking people up when they "feel like it" doesn't appeal to them.

Time passes slowly and years can go by without anything very emotionally exciting happening. Those who have an interesting professional life get through these phases better. Those who like to read, study, or spend time with their few genuine friends are also in a privileged situation. Those who are more reserved or whose professional or intellectual lives are not very stimulating suffer a lot. They should make an effort to find some kind of entertainment, as this is a resource that depends only on them. Finding love is fortuitous and random.

**Suddenly, when they least expect it, they meet an interesting person who seems to want approximation. They have those intimate conversations that are so rare and yearned for. They realize they have a lot in common (character, points of view, tastes) and similar difficulties. They feel understood, as if the other were able to decode their words exactly as they were intended to be read. They feel cosy! Finding someone who thinks and feels as they do makes them feel less alone.**

This is the point when people start thinking about "soul mates" and think they have met in "past lives". It is as if they can communicate by telepathy: one says precisely what the other is thinking. They tell each other the stories of their lives, and, in this uncommon experience, there are no judgements. Their reciprocal trust grows and the confidences become more detailed. They get to know one another radically and deeply. They each feel accepted by someone who knows everything about their past, their small sins, their foibles and insecurities.

**Intimacy grows in a similar way for both. Now we are really talking about bilateral involvement. It is cosiness, the moment they have dreamed of, the warmth of really being with someone; someone who is present body and soul. They want for nothing else; time could stop for all they care.** When they are together, time flies and hours seem like minutes. Other people cease to exist. There is nothing outside of the wonderful feeling of completeness. They feel love — in its fullest sense — for that special someone who awakens such delightful feelings. The pain of parting is immense. They think constantly and obsessively about what is happening and nothing they used to be interested in is relevant any more.

Parting is accompanied by brutal insecurities, doubts about what the other one feels, if they still want them, how long it will be before they get in touch. People lose their appetites and get only a minimum amount of sleep. Their hearts beat fast and hard — out of fear![15] Every

---

**15** The racing hearts typical of love are actually motivated by fear. It is not an indication of emotional intensity; rather, the intensity of one's fear.

phone call (or other kind of contact) abates their fear for a few minutes. Seeing the person abates it a little more. But insecurity rears its head again every time they have to say goodbye, which is unavoidable. **Fears are an integral part of the process of falling in love. The first — and most immediate — is of being abandoned.**

twenty six

**I define passionate** love as the emotional cosiness derived from a good quality, intense relationship coupled with an equal measure of fear. Passionate love = love + fear. The first fear, as I said in the last chapter, is of losing what we have finally found and fallen for. It is not the only one, and tends to lessen as time goes by. Our fear of abandonment diminishes as lovers reassure one another of the reciprocity and stability of the feeling that unites them.

Another fear that comes into play here has to do with the phenomenon of romantic fusion. Meeting a person with whom we feel intensely connected provokes a strong feeling that we have finally found our "missing half". The feeling of incompleteness that accompanies us from birth stems from the disruption of our original symbiotic relationship, and we believe — due to the way we learn to think about love — that we will only feel complete again when, as adults, we find what we think we are missing.

We can assume that this is an adult union, because "fusion" is a sign of a more mature relationship, based on character and intellectual affinities. Such affinities also

give rise to the feeling of cosiness typical of friendships. **The combination of physical and intellectual cosiness can bring on a brutal and terrifying attraction: people feel profoundly threatened in their individuality. This is where the traditional antagonism between love and individuality peaks. The connection is wonderful and irresistible. The only reason people's individuality isn't so threatened that they break it off is because of their strong affinities, which determine an acceptable amount of concessions. In other words, in spite of the intensity of fusion, the limitations on the lovers' identity are tolerable.**

But these limitations are only just tolerable, such that the fear can sometimes be quite intense. A good example is when two lovers have the opportunity to spend a longer period of time together. They feel as if they are being suffocated, wearing clothes that are too tight around the neck. It gets harder to breathe, and time away from their lover, although painful, is experienced with great relief. Those who live in different cities are benefited by the compulsory distancing dictated by the need to go back to their daily lives.

**Fear of passionate love has to do with a) the fear of ruptured ties; b) the threat to people's hard-won individuality; and c) the fear of happiness. It is a strange feeling of foreboding and imminent tragedy that assails people every time they feel particularly happy because of an achievement.** Nothing provokes this diffuse fear — which appears as if with the wave of a magic wand — more than and as intensely as falling in love.

People become incredibly superstitious when they are happy. They say things like "this happiness can't last forever," or "it's too good to be true." They feel as if some kind of tragedy were lying in wait for those who find themselves in a truly satisfying relationship.

I shall return soon to the topic of the fear of happiness and its destructive tendencies (which give rise to involuntary acts whose underlying intention is to place a distance between the person and the plenitude they experience as threatening), which I have written about on numerous occasions. **Here I shall merely state that lovers live in a state of emergency, as if they were in a battlefield where they might get hit at any moment. It is thus no wonder they become obsessed with their situation and have such great difficulty concentrating on their daily obligations.**

**People in love live in an "extraordinary state"** (to cite the felicitous expression Francesco Alberoni uses in *Falling in Love*[16]). **They feel unique, special, as if they were experiencing something extremely rare — which, curiously, is actually repetitive and standardized. They live as if the strong feelings of fear were a part of the romantic nature of the relationship, and don't realize that their love stories are more like horror films, in which dangerous spirits haunt them constantly. They love and suffer as they do in few other situations. In spite of all the pain and fear, they never regret the situation, and feel that now their lives finally make sense!**

---

[16] ALBERONI, Francesco, *Falling in Love*. New York: Random House, 1983.

twenty seven

**I have been thinking** and writing about passionate love since 1970. Something that has always intrigued me was the fact that such an intense feeling — always between people who are similar in many essential aspects, as is also the case in friendships — almost invariably manifests in situations where there are obstacles that are insurmountable or very hard to resolve. Even today the kind of intense involvement typical of passionate love between uncommitted, available people is rare.

There are many hypotheses that attempt to explain this fact, also present in the literature on love for many centuries. Some have to do with practical considerations that came to bear on the choice of partners until not very long ago: families used to arrange marriages between young people, and marriages of convenience didn't fulfil people's need for love and were supposed to last a lifetime. Intense, extramarital involvements thus became par for the course. Psychoanalytical theories point to triangular childhood problems (Oedipal) that seek another attempt at resolution in adult life (the thesis put forward by Igor Caruso, an Austrian psychoanalyst who published a pioneering work on the subject in 1968 called *Die Trennung der Liebenden* [Love and Separation][17]).

**The undeniable fact is that the obstacles used to be practically insurmountable, such that the tragic destiny of passionate love affairs was present in the minds of lovers throughout the entire process of falling in love. They had a wonderful feeling of completeness when they were together, but at the same time it was almost certain that the relationship would have an extremely painful end. Many such stories ended with the lovers committing suicide, unable to overcome external obstacles or imagine life without one another.**

The impediments were diverse: marriages to other people, in times and cultures in which divorce was unthinkable; intolerable racial and religious differences; rivalry and divergences between the families of young lovers; dramatic differences in age or place of residence. Only the most daring couples — bordering on irresponsible — were willing to break with tradition and deeply hurt others who were emotionally important to them. Since people who fall in love tend to worry about the rights of others, they feel guilt and, in the past, they were probably emotionally unprepared to do something so radical, even in the name of the most intensely passionate love. They would rather suffer personally, for example, than hurt their mother and father.

---

**17** Sadly, not available in English.

**Flávio Gikovate**

But times have changed. Divorce is now common in most countries. Only very religious cultures are against marriages between people of different creeds. Age differences are more readily accepted by all. Geographical problems are almost always resolvable. Families interfere less and less in people's choice of spouse. One would expect that, with fewer external obstacles, most people who fell in love would do whatever they had to do, as quickly as possible, so that they could be with the people they love, thus realizing the romantic dream they crave and consider so important.

If only! **Even today the vast majority of those who fall deeply in love do not make their satisfying relationships into something real, a single, committed union. They dream of marriage as they always have. In the past it didn't happen because of external obstacles, but nowadays, even with no prohibition, they dream without making it come true!** The saddest part is that they still attribute the non-consummation of the relationship to the same obstacles, now so easy to overcome: married people use their children as an "alibi" for not leaving spouses they don't love (if they loved them, they wouldn't fall in love with someone else). I have heard women say, to justify staying in an unhappy marriage, that they wouldn't have to courage to separate their children from their father. I won't even comment on the other obstacles mentioned, as it is obvious that they don't have the relevance attributed to them and that they are only being used as a shield.

# A Love Story...
**Flávio Gikovate**

Four decades have passed and I have accompanied hundreds of stories of passionate love that ended in painful and unnecessary separation. A few, of course, were successful, and the lovers had the courage to continue the relationship. My conviction is stronger than ever, and what I have always suspected is confirmed with each new case I see: the obstacle to fulfilment in love is internal! Much greater weight needs to be attributed to the fears I have described. The fear of the pain of separation, the fear of losing one's individuality, and the fear of happiness make up a potent "antilove factor", which wins most battles. External obstacles have always existed and should not be overlooked. But it seems they are easier to overcome than those inside us.

## twenty eight

**I would like** to give some more thought to the antilove factor, since it is very powerful and influential in our emotional lives. **It is important to note that it grows in proportion to the intensity of love! The less intense the love, the less intense the antilove factor. It reaches its peak in passionate love. It makes sense, because the fear of fusion increases as the possibility of it happening grows.**

Couples who get along very well, who love one another intensely and reciprocally, in addition to having similar habits and character traits naturally lean toward fusion, which is what we all dream of. If they also like the way the other one walks, talks, and smiles (which I call the "X factor": the sum of countless, unspecified factors that are essential in order for there to be attraction), they feel increasingly defenceless against this craving that accompanies us from birth. Everything conspires so that they can't stay away from one another for more than a few hours — exactly like what happens in the relationship between a newborn baby and its mother.

The regressive nature of this tendency toward fusion is undeniable. Even the words lovers use to address one another (sweetie, cutie, honey etc.) are the same as those mothers use to address their young children. **Our psychology is curious indeed: we are irritated by differences, but at the same time they save us from fusion. This important factor leads us to make inadequate choices, which mean a lower risk of fusion. Our lovers' qualities (read "the things we like about them") attract us, while their flaws repel us. It is obvious that we really need our partners' flaws because they protect us from fusion.**

When they have few flaws (read: "different points of view or behaviour"), we're in trouble, and the antilove factor is at its highest. Our individuality is profoundly threatened, since romantic fusion is its biggest and most dangerous enemy. We over-exaggerate the importance and weight of external obstacles, which, in this case, compensate the flaws we are unable to attribute to our lovers. We cling to them in the hope that they will impede the union we desire and fear so much (generally the fear outweighs the desire).

Fear of happiness is a feeling of imminent tragedy that lurks around us in our best moments. It is as if the great tragedy is about to happen again. We were in our mother's womb, happy, in harmony and symbiosis with our mothers, and then the paradisiacal situation was disrupted by the dramatic and painful separation of birth. We are left with a kind of conditioning, such that whenever we are in harmony, happy and serene, we feel as if a new tragedy were about to happen, now associated with the idea of death. What do we do? We

look for a way to free ourselves of that blissful happiness. We find all manner of ways to destroy the plenitude, at least in part, in order to protect ourselves. We voluntarily give up part of what we have with the objective of preserving what we think is essential.

Love is the biggest driving force behind our happiness (and is also directly related to our earliest experiences, the same ones that gave rise to the conditioning described above), and the fear that something terrible is going to happen is tremendous. We find ways to fight and sabotage the relationship, always with the intention of avoiding a more dramatic form of destruction. We often destroy more than we need to and seek out the topics that most cause us sadness and suffering. Lovers who dream of being together often torture themselves for hours on end thinking of supposedly insurmountable obstacles and imagining the suffering that they are going to have to inflict on others. They spend much of the scarce time they have together discussing what will become of them in the dark future.

The brutal threat to lovers' individuality and the feeling that death is lurking just around the corner (occasioned by fear of emotional happiness) join forces and lead to dramatic break-ups. The beginning of quality relationships is disturbed by the fear of suffering inherent in the possibility of a break-up. This is, in fact, what ends up happening, and it is quite likely that it makes many people cower at the thought of a new intense involvement. The opposite can also happen: when they realize that they are able to tolerate this pain — one of the greatest anyone may ever experience — they may feel strong and courageous enough to embark on new romantic adventures.

**The depression and pain experienced in the lovers' separation is the pain of death: it is knowing that we are dying in the other person's mind. Dying in their mind and killing them in ours. The recovery period is long, and some may never get over it. Many lovers meet up again years — or decades — later and can't see one another with neutrality. The "magic" of love makes someone "neutral" unique and indispensable. Separation should reverse this "magic", returning the special person to the condition of mere mortal. This doesn't always happen.**

**What happens** to a person's subjectivity after they know what it is to feel passionate love? This is a crucial experience in the story of their love lives. Their outlook will probably never be the same again. I think there are four different outcomes: 1) many people give up on the hope of living out a great love story and settle into a relationship — existing or future — of less intensity and quality; 2) another large contingency of people are strengthened by the experience and are willing to give it another try, now with more awareness and the courage to see it through; 3) a small number of couples refuse to accept the idea of separation and try to overcome the obstacles posed by the antilove factor (I will come to them shortly); 4) another small group of people conclude that love is a regressive phenomenon and an unbearable threat to their individuality — and make a definitive choice in favour of the latter.

Those who, like myself, have accompanied many love stories know that passionate love is a turning point. The selfish, who have a low frustration threshold, don't usually fall in love. They represent half of the population and prefer not to take many risks in this area, precisely because they know they are unprepared to deal with suffering, should it arise. They stay in the "comfortable" condition of those who are loved, the object of the dedication of more generous sorts, who are also too immature for real love, because that would imply reciprocity. As well as not taking any risks, the selfish take for granted the "privileged" condition of those who reap advantages and still complain. They are not very trustworthy and entertain themselves by stimulating the emotional and erotic interest of other people — with whom they may start a superficial, uncommitted relationship on the side. They lead their lives in this manner, but deep down they envy those who fall in love and have the courage to plunge headlong into the delights and horrors of it all. Of course they will never recognize this envy, just as they are unlikely to recognize that — due to the time spent together — they are more attached to their generous partners than they care to be. They establish relationships of practical dependence, in which they accept being waited upon and also end up depending emotionally on their partners, which always happens when we share day-to-day life with someone. They feign emotional nonchalance and threaten separation at the drop of a hat. If and when it actually happens, however, they become desperate and experience all the pain that they have tried so hard to avoid. Pain also assails those who fear it!

Generous people who are unable to recover from the experience of failed passionate love are condemned to a

rather dark destiny. They will have moments of great sadness for many years, especially when they realize that they took the initiative to pull away from their loved one motivated by fear. Those who think they were rejected or abandoned may also feel dreadful, but they won't carry the burden of cowardice — which they had actually managed to tame, in spite of the fact that they also felt great fear. Some people think that one only finds passionate love once in a lifetime, and thus consider any failure irreparable. They accept a mediocre emotional life, see it as part of their sad destiny, and seek compensation in other family relationships, especially with their children. Sometimes they channel their energy into social or professional activities in an attempt to obtain the gratification that has become impossible on an emotional level.

**The more selfish sorts, plus those who back down when faced with the problems involving passionate love and its pain, make up the majority — perhaps as much as 75% — of the population. They have already lost the chance to finish travelling this extremely difficult path that leads to happy endings in love. Those who have been hurt and frustrated, but who have managed to recover, stay in the fight.** They have learned the true intensity of the pain of loving. They have learned, at least in part, to see where they went wrong. They may have begun to familiarize themselves with the role of the antilove factor and the need to respect it both in themselves and their partners. They are certain-

ly in a better position to try again. They depend on the appearance of a new appropriate partner, which can be somewhat random. If the opportunity arises, however, they will try again and their chances of success will be much bigger than the first time around.

# 30 thirty

**I would like** to make a few brief observations about those who have fallen in love, realized the strength of the tendency toward fusion when their partner is very compatible, and concluded that it was not in accordance with their deepest convictions. After all, love can sometimes require changes to a person's plans that they are not prepared to make. A simple example of the problem is a doctor who dreams of doing missionary work (with, say, Doctors Without Borders) and falls in love with someone who has more urban dreams. The impossibility of accommodating both sets of serious individual dreams within a relationship is clear and makes life in common unviable.

**I think the fear of love related to the fear of suffering as a result of a separation is perfectly surmountable. I think the same about the fear of emotional happiness, because it doesn't increase our real risks at all. However, there is no doubt that real problems exist for those who want both love and individuality.** In many cases, such as the above example, it is a real dilemma. The antagonism between love and individuality has two possible solutions: the first is to try to learn to be OK on one's own. And I shall come to the second shortly.

Solving this dilemma is crucial in order for love stories to have happy endings, and **I see two possible outcomes. A happy ending means full satisfaction. I am not talking about intermediate solutions, like "first a little love, then a little individuality." Nor am I thinking of the painful renouncement of one or the other. When we are in a loving relationship, we miss our individuality, and vice-versa.**

It is interesting to consider what is most important: love or individuality. Although the answer now seems evident, the vast majority of people will still say that there is nothing more sacred and important than love. They still have an idealized vision of love and a completely distorted idea of what it means to be alone — which they consider a terrible condition. They still think it is better to be in an unsatisfactory relationship than alone!

I have repeatedly tried to point out the connection between the phenomenon of love and the pain of forsakenness that we feel from the moment we are born. Maternal care is the remedy for this pain, and love is what we feel for our mother. With time, and as we gain confidence, we start to exercise our individuality by trying to understand everything around us. We entertain ourselves more and more with this continuous learning and only return to our mothers when we feel insecure.

The similarities between adult love and these processes are obvious. The differences are the sex and conversational and intellectual preferences — the same as we have with our friends. We want someone to look after us when we are in pain or sick, just like when we were children; "adult" nights are problematic, such that we like to sleep in our lovers' arms, it is harder to cook a proper meal for one, and we feel socially insecure and weak when we are not in somebody else's company.

**With the exception of sex and occasionally — very occasionally — friendship, what is left is a dependency on one's partner, who now substitutes our mother, to attenuate our feelings of forsakenness. "Adult love" is that!** This dependency is what gives rise to jealousy, consenting possessiveness, the fear of losing or being away from our partner, of being traded in for someone else. Dependency generates such a great fear of separation that people are even prepared to tolerate rude or disrespectful behaviour from their partners. Because love is a feeling that unites us with another person above all because we are not entirely self-sufficient, it is obvious why we are so willing to make such great sacrifices and concessions in its name.

Some people observe these phenomena critically from a young age. They watch what happens in their own homes, to friends and relatives, and can even develop an aversion to relationships. I don't think it is ideal, but I do think it is more typical of selfish types and different to fear of love. In these cases, they seek self-sufficiency — rather than someone to exploit. People adverse to relationships seek to become better and better at doing everything on their own. They try to find other kinds of relief for feelings of forsaken-

ness. They try to attenuate it themselves instead of running to someone's arms — which to them is very threatening.

What do they do? I know many who are extremely dedicated to their professions, as well as having a host of other activities to keep them occupied as much as possible in their free time. They play sports, read, watch films, and have other intellectual activities. They keep their heads busy, because they feel less pain this way. Little by little they manage to "tame" the "hole" we all feel in our stomachs. They learn to live with this unpleasant feeling when, in spite of everything, it appears. After all, our condition really is that of the forsaken!

Those who are more extroverted seek social solutions: they have many friendships, which they cultivate with great fondness. Some become quite intimate, which gives them a pleasant feeling of intellectual cosiness typical of relationships based on sincerity and loyalty. They participate actively in community life and are more available for parties and activities at sports and recreational clubs.

Both introverts and extroverts seek autonomy and independence. They respect their nature and entertain themselves in accordance with it. They may have romantic and sexual partners, although the more sociable ones find it a lot easier. Their relationships tend not to be very committed and they don't include plans for a future in common; at least on their part. Their partners often don't believe it and end up disappointed.

Their plans are individual and generally short-term. Daily life is good for them. There will be the inevitable setbacks and illnesses, and then, perhaps, they might miss having a more stable partner. But there will always be close friends and relatives who can fulfil their basic needs. After all, not even the most solitary are that solitary. On the other hand, I don't see the point in a couple merely tolerating one another with the objective of having someone to lean on in hours of need.

**People on their own who are psychologically comfortable with their single status and can deal with the pains of living get by very well. They can enjoy all manner of intellectual pleasure, have friends they can count on, and are free to have a rich sex life and good emotional bonds. They don't suffer the limitations of possessive relationships nor the need to reconcile interests — inevitable even in the best relationships. They suffer less, live in peace, and have access to many moments of happiness. They can actually be very happy — no matter how sceptical their peers might be.**

# 31

thirty one

**Many people** who are able to cope with the pain of forsakenness — therefore competent at being alone — may fall head over heels in love when they meet someone special. This can happen to a diehard individualist or someone who is single (or unhappily married and aware of it) and yearning for this moment. The former will be surprised and, to an extent, terrified. The latter will feel that happiness is finally knocking at their door.

**Individualists, who were happy with their single lives to this point, are strongly shaken in their convictions. They baulk and have a hard time adjusting. There is no way to tell if they will give up the intense involvement or try to reformulate their lives. The choice depends a lot on the peculiarities of their lives, as well as the kind of person they have met.** It will also depend on whether they are certain that if the relationship goes ahead it won't affect their hard-won individuality (a source of important pleasures) too much. **It is a golden dilemma: both options are attractive and offer excellent perspectives for the future.**

Those who yearned for a bilateral relationship — and the individualists who chose involvement — will be, in

**Flávio Gikovate**

a matter days, in a state similar to that described in chapters 25 and 26: in love and experiencing the feeling of fusion, of becoming one, of the same flesh (as described in *Genesis*). Obviously, in this context, one can't think about individuality. If it was well established, it will now seem as if it is about to dissolve forever. The fusion is total and experienced as highly gratifying. Fears aren't predominant, but they are there. Thus, fusion also feels threatening (fear of happiness), asphyxiating (due to the loss of one's individuality), and unstable (because of the fear of separation, which quickly becomes essential).

We feel as if we don't need anything else, that our old interests are irrelevant, that material things are superfluous, that the moment is sublime and should last forever. This doesn't happen, since life doesn't stop just because lovers want it to. If a couple gets serious about living out their romantic fusion fully and exclusively, abandoning everything and moving to a cottage in the forest, they will most certainly be disappointed. The love that unites people is a source of cosiness, but it isn't entertaining enough for minds used to action.

Full romantic fusion implies a kind of return to the womb! When we were foetuses, our mind was devoid of information (naïve and free of anxiety), prepared to live in this paradisiacal condition. When we are grown, we lose our naivety, bite into the fruit of knowledge, and can no longer tolerate Paradise — which becomes monotonous, repetitive, boring! **In a nutshell: full fu-**

sion and its transformation into a reason to live is an unexpected fiasco.

Fortunately, most couples don't usually take this path. People in love dream of a paradisiacal life together but have to keep working, attending family events, dealing with practical matters, etc. They may not like it, but they don't know how much worse it would be if their dream were to come true. In spite of the limitations imposed by reality, they live for one another, are less available for their friends (now seen as less important), talk to one another several times a day, and know each other's every-move. People who until now had bragged of their independence undergo unimaginable lifestyle changes.

**Hitherto independent people now feel extremely neglected if, for a few moments, their lover doesn't treat them like the most important thing on the face of the earth. They are jealous of anything and everything, of children and pets. They are jealous of the life the other led before they met. Their jealousy is retroactive! They wish they were the other person's sole reason for living, as if they had come directly from the womb into their arms.** Such feelings reaffirm the regressive nature of passionate love in the cases in which it is consummated: they are as possessive and jealous as young children are of their mothers.

Lovers' discourse is monotonous and repetitive, but it fuels people's vanity because it is reciprocal. "You are the most wonderful person alive," "I couldn't live without you," and a handful of other phrases are trotted out time

and time again. If babies could talk, these are the things they would say to their mothers. This fuelling of their vanity is satisfying enough to substitute all other sources of recognition and prestige, at least for a time. This is yet another reason why couples tend to isolate themselves, because in this sense they are self-sufficient.

**The suffocating and somewhat obsessive nature of the relationship wanes as the months go by. Apart from that, everything else remains the same for some years. Lovers are idealized; their "flaws", overlooked. The fear of separation diminishes, as does the fear of happiness. They may at times miss their individuality, but because the affinities are many and the differences minimal, their happiness outweighs any resentment.**

# thirty two

**I would like to make** some important observations about sex in the context of passionate love. **It is evident to me that sexuality operates in the arena of individuality — rather than romantic fusion.** Sex is a personal phenomenon, activated by the discovery of erogenous zones at the end of our first year of life. In puberty, it takes on the appearance of an interpersonal phenomenon because boys start to discover that their arousal is visually stimulated and because women become aroused when they realize they are desired.

**Most sexual problems in passionate love manifest in men. The most common is erectile dysfunction, a phenomenon caused by countless factors. The most immediate is that whenever a man greatly admires a woman, he tends to feel inferior to her. This is because he needs her acquiescence in order to approach her, which, from his point of view, gives her the upper hand, sexually speaking. As a result, he needs to feel superior to her intellectually and emotionally to level the playing field. It might be hard for the woman to grasp, but for him, the simple fact that he desires her more than he thinks he is desired in return makes him feel sexually inferior.**

**Flávio Gikovate**

Freud wrote about this need of men to feel superior to women in order to feel sexually confident.[18] Some are only able to desire women who are inferior, while others just need to feel equal to them. When they fall in love, they tend to idealize their partners, putting them up on a pedestal. Male self-esteem is usually lower than people imagine. As such, even when they are equal, a man will feel inferior and, as a result, sexually impaired.

The connection between sex and individuality also plays an important role in inhibiting desire: when the man's psychological defences against falling in love weaken, his erectile dysfunction points to the fact that there is still internal resistance to romantic fusion. This resistance is more than justified, because it indicates the importance of his individuality and the size of the threat. Thus, while the man is trying to work out whether or not he is as good as the woman who so enchants him and deciding if he is going to allow himself to be drawn into romantic fusion, he remains sexually blocked.

Women tend to explain what is happening differently and don't even consider the above hypothesis, which is actually a compliment, seeing as sexually healthy men only have problems with partners they are very attracted to. They seriously entertain the thought that they are not attractive enough and fear that the relationship will end because it is not sexually interesting.

---

**18** FREUD, Sigmund. "On the Universal Tendency to Debasement in the Sphere of Love." 1912.

**As a result, they sometimes set out to prove that they are more competent and uninhibited in this area, which only makes life more difficult for the men, who feel pressured.** Men's sexual insecurities are enormous and shouldn't be underestimated. It doesn't take much for them to worry about their sexual performance, which aggravates the problem a lot. In other words, what was at first essentially a question of working out if he was as good as the woman and willing to risk his individuality in a relationship can become a bugbear, a concern that detracts from his spontaneity even after the initial causes of the erectile dysfunction are gone.

Except for the anxiety related to the fear of physically disappointing their partners, women experience sexual intimacy in the context of passionate love much more serenely than men do. As a matter of fact, many actually feel safer letting go in this romantic setting because they are sure their sensuality won't overflow the limits of that relationship. **A common fear among women is that if they let themselves go too much sexually they will lose control of themselves; this fear disappears when the romantic atmosphere is at a peak.**

**Men also have another difficulty: visual arousal depends on the woman's exteriority. In other words, in romantic fusion the man feels as if the woman were part of him, a condition that puts a damper on arousal.**[19] As if these difficulties weren't enough, many men have

---

[19] Plato said, "If you don't lack it, you can't desire it."

learned to associate sex with violence rather than love. This explains why so many men need sex to be "dirty" rather than romantic.

In psychology, there are always countless exceptions. But most of the time the sexual arousal of men in love normalizes as they feel less fear of failure, which usually happens when they belief they are as good as their partner. When they come to the opposite conclusion, they bail out, because they will never recover from their erectile dysfunction in this situation — which women, obviously, have a hard time believing. Sex improves even more when couples realize that romantic ingredients don't always have to be a part of it; on the contrary, somewhat vulgar words and clothes may be more fitting to the occasion.

**This subtraction of romanticism from the erotic context creates interesting conditions, because the woman goes back to being "any" woman for a few minutes. She is no longer part of the man, recovers her integrality, and becomes a female of the species (which may also be very exciting for her). In this case arousal may come flooding back in all its intensity. It may even become somewhat frightening, especially for women, since the men take the refractory period[20] as a breather.**

---

[20] This term was coined by Masters and Johnson, who pioneered research into the human sexual response from 1957 until the early 1990's. They found that men undergo a refractory period following orgasm during which they are not able to ejaculate again. Women experience no such period.

At any rate, we are looking at the full expression of sexuality that takes place in the context of romantic fusion. Sexual pleasure is individual and solitary, and there is no reason why we should go on dreaming of the traditional ideal that holds that pleasure should always be simultaneous. **When we climax, we close our eyes and allow ourselves to be completely washed over by our own sensations. For instants, the other person — and the rest of the world — disappears. We are swept away on a wave of pleasure and when the few seconds of total ecstasy are over we recognize our partner again and embrace them with urgency and pleasure.**

**What comes next is a magical moment, a reunion! It is comforting to lie in our lover's arms, now wrapped in tenderness. Sexual arousal has gone and tenderness has returned.** Men, now relaxed thanks to the refractory period, sleep like babies, serene and confident — which doesn't happen to women, who don't have an automatic "off" button for sexual arousal. Perhaps because their experience of the moment is different, they have a hard time seeing that this is indeed proof of the man's love. When a man sleeps with someone in whom he is only interested sexually, he still feels alone and goes to great lengths to extricate himself from the situation as quickly as possible.

# 33 thirty three

**The months** — and sometimes years — go by and the balance between love and individuality gradually changes: the romantic fusion loses its strength, while individuality requires more and more space. This is due to countless factors, but perhaps the strongest is that love is the remedy for forsakenness. The cosy, successful relationship works like an "incubator", a complement to the womb and maternal love. Thus, the incompleteness that we feel from the moment we are born is diminished. We need less and less "maternal protection" and feel increasingly disposed to individual adventures.

Little by little we start to recognize — with renewed surprise — the limitations of love. The promised plenitude tends to become a monotonous repetition of phrases, gestures, and actions. Spending time with our lover is still wonderful, but the ins and outs of sentimental happiness become somewhat uninteresting. They are no longer enough, as they once were. **Suddenly, one of the two verbalizes what both are feeling: they need more space for their individuality, for their personal projects. They want a part of their life to be just theirs!**

**Flávio Gikovate**

It is a cry of independence, a declaration against love. It indicates a certain disappointment with the romantic scenario. It is the opposite of everything that has been done, said, and thought over the years. It is curious because, even though it is a mutual feeling, it seems to catch the partners off guard.

It is one thing to think something; another to voice it out loud; and quite another to hear it! I must admit that beyond this point in relationships, my clinical experience is far more limited. Most people are in relationships with their opposites, which could lead to growth but usually don't. The more generous sometimes experience passionate love, and most of these stories end with the separation of the lovers. Of those who separate, most fall back into old patterns, while some decide to live alone. Some are fine like this, and most hope for another opportunity at love. Few ever experience fusion, and the ones who do rarely seek specialists, because they live happily for many years. Those who sense the fragility of this fusion are even fewer, such that the sample group only decreases. I have no other choice but to resort to personal experience and stories told in certain films and novels (such as the film *Elvira Madigan*[21] and the book *Belle du Seigneur*[22]).

---

[21] A 1967 Swedish film, directed by Bo Widerberg, which tells the true story of an army officer who abandons his career, wife and children when he falls passionately in love with a circus performer. They experience many hardships, lose all hope in the future, and come to see death as the only way out.

[22] Albert Cohen's 1968 novel *Belle du Seigneur* (published in English as *Her Lover*), considered a literary masterpiece, tells the story of an intense love affair. After breaking taboos and social rules, the lovers run away together to live in isolation, but what used to be passionate love turns into disappointment.

**Flávio Gikovate**

**I am fully convinced that romantic fusion should not be considered an end in itself. We can't go on thinking of love as the remedy for all ills, the formula that takes us back to the perpetual serenity of Paradise.** We need to free ourselves of the belief — so strong in our culture — that love unlocks all of the doors to happiness. Because of the acquisition of language and the advances that are the fruit of our intellectual restlessness, we are not moved by a feeling of incompleteness alone. Incompleteness is attenuated by romantic fusion; but our intellectual restlessness continues. If this ideal romance means limiting our intellectual activity, the overwhelming feeling will be one of boredom.

Intellectual restlessness is a personal phenomenon, but romantic partners will probably share many topics of interest. There will, however, always be topics that only one is interested in. We have our own thought system that identifies us, and we can't give it up indefinitely — hence the cry of independence when our feeling of incompleteness is reduced by the strength of love. The person who heard the cry may at first feel offended, betrayed. It is as if they have been abandoned. The one who lets out the cry is surprised by their lover's reaction, since the intention was merely to loosen the romantic tie that had become suffocating. **Everything is surprising, because who could have thought that the dream relationship could lead to dissatisfaction, causing their individuality to lash out so dramatically?**

In spite of their drastic reaction, as if they were deeply offended by this attitude so contrary to love, I think lovers take the opportunity to make even more individualistic decisions. It is as if they were anxiously awaiting a chance to recover a little of themselves, since they were also tired of being half of the original androgyne described in Plato's *The Symposium*.

**These are surprising movements and clearly indicate the victory of individuality over romantic love — which is the fusion of two halves.** The result is unexpected, since we learn that love is the supreme source of happiness and all things good. This paradigm seems to derive from a regressive point of view: we spend most of our adult lives trying to recover something we lost at birth — and which grows worse the more independent we become. **It is as if our individual and social history was that of those who are unwilling to accept birth, their expulsion from Paradise, the fact that life is the way it is. It seems we only seek alternative remedies for this pain, instead of examining the construction of our history — which in this sense hasn't even begun.**

We adults are just like children who want our mothers' warm embrace — now substituted by our lover — all the time. We think it is the be-all and end-all and it is our greatest desire! This is our big (rather pathetic) goal in life and we forget to take into consideration that children themselves, after the age of two, tire of pure cosiness, climb down from their mothers' arms, and go live life (their mothers' arms are prelife). They only return when

# A Love Story...
**Flávio Gikovate**

they feel threatened. We have very active, gifted brains that generate a restlessness that doesn't allow us to live out this paradisiacal dream. (Perhaps it is better suited to dogs, from whom dozing next to their beloved masters seems to be the best thing in the world — at least when they are not perturbed by instinctive processes.)

**No matter how paradoxical it seems, a love story with a truly happy ending implies the death of love! Not the death of those who love one another, as in literature, but the death of this childish, immature way of trying to resolve the issue of forsakenness, a residue of our lost symbiosis.** The happy ending involves accepting that this loss really is permanent and that there is no use looking for apparently ingenious alternatives — such as romantic love.

Most people don't have the courage to embark upon this almost irresponsible regressive adventure. They have their reasons! However, it isn't for the right reasons that they don't do it, but fear, such that they continue dreaming about what they haven't done. We are lucky that some have had the courage to take the plunge. **They have come back with excellent tidings. They don't teach us that love is a wonderful, definitive experience. They come back with big news, a new paradigm: it is essential that we abandon our pathetic dream and seek solutions that involve growth, compatible with the fact that we are adults.**

# 34
thirty four

**The end of love** as we know it is auspicious news. Many tears have been shed and many fights have been had in the name of love, in addition to more radical cases of homicide and suicide. Not to mention those who suffer because they don't have someone to love. Those who are successful in love have always been few in number. And it is from them that I bring the news that fusion offends people's individuality to such an extent that it makes no sense to go on dreaming of and striving for something that doesn't work so well.

Technological advances have actually incited our individuality even more. MP3 players, computers, DVDs, children's games: all of these things afford us good solitary entertainment from a young age. We are becoming better and better at being on our own, having fun with technology, and few of us are willing to make major concessions in favour of traditional love, which is demanding and full of pressures to do things we don't want to.

These socio-cultural reasons help us to understand the oppressive aspects of love and to grow emotionally. We are increasingly competent at living alone, and it is this reinforcement of individualism that has enabled us to observe the phenomenon with other eyes. We can no longer think of people who are not in a relationship as unhappy and solitary. Many people choose to live this way. They prefer to face and learn to live with the feeling of incompleteness — always much less when we are entertained — than make the concessions typical of demanding, possessive love.

When they systematically confront the pain of forsakenness that manifests above all when people are unoccupied, they learn that it isn't that bad. Managing to deal with the feeling of incompleteness is an extraordinary psychological step forward. It opens highly interesting doors for the building of an original lifestyle in which traditional norms — much less value judgements — are no longer valid. **If we are able to look at it without bias, we will see that solitude can be rich, pleasurable, and liberating. It may be just a phase of adult life or it could last forever. It may alternate with periods of interesting emotional involvement — which will always be less oppressive.** Those who have tasted freedom tend not to relinquish it, except temporarily (as happens with passionate love).

**In the case of more intense relationships, in which the couple has much in common in terms of moral values, lifestyle, tastes, and intellectual interests, the individualistic about-turn doesn't usually affect the friendship between those who participated in the romantic fusion.** They will probably feel temporarily hurt as a result of the "separatist" words they heard from one who was supposedly happy with way things were. I would like to stress, however, that the need for individual freedom characteristic of the end of the "dark" phase of fusion is reciprocal, as long as both grow emotionally in a similar way. They are "cured" of their immaturity more or less at the same time. **What happens is that things get better and the friendship is strengthened. This is because they were partners in an unusual adventure, privileged survivors of a risky voyage to the depths of the soul.** Their shared history is rich, and the friendship only gains from it. In addition to the romantic side of things, they have usually built lives together. They are more than enough reasons to stay together. **Their individual experiences grow, but there is still a very important "us", strong enough to for them to see the future as a couple.**

Individuated people can play the "game of life" individually or as a couple. The couple is now the approximation of two individuals, rather than their fusion "as one flesh" and one being. There will always be an important area of intersection — an "us" — and an area of "me" in each. **When they want to and have the opportunity, they are together. When they don't, they follow their own paths. This type of alliance, defined by friendship (affinity of character and thought), respect for individuality (and their inevitable differences), and shared plans is much more sophisticated than traditional love** — based on the idea that love unites and gives meaning to people's lives.

# A Love Story...
**Flávio Gikovate**

Love is just a palliative remedy for the pain of forsakenness and doesn't actually bestow meaning on anything. Because it alleviates suffering, it is a negative pleasure. **Friendship and individual projects are positive pleasures, which (associated with a satisfying sex life — also a positive pleasure), are part of a new kind of alliance between lovers. I am convinced that this is a great advance and that there is nothing to lament about the end of love — and the enormous suffering that has always accompanied it. Those who have emotionally grown toward individuality are equipped to experience something that is more than love. I call this phenomenon love+.**

# 35
thirty five

**Even when we are living love+**, the residues of emotional dependence typical of love reappear due to the intimacy of the relationship and inevitable moments of weakness. Aware adults recognize this regressive tendency that haunts us throughout life and which we need to resist always. **In moments of physical illness or when something shakes us emotionally (after all, just because someone is mature it doesn't mean they are a superhero!) we are more susceptible to regression and take a few steps back temporarily. We shouldn't beat ourselves up over it, as these moments are inevitable. Besides, we make up the lost ground as soon as our energies are back to normal.**

The most notable difference is in how we view dependence: in love, it is worshipped and treated as a blessing; the same thing happens with one of its most terrible sub-products, jealousy, considered proof of the intensity and sincerity of love. In couples who have attained love+, the vestige of emotional dependence is treated as an inevitable "scar", as a vestige of something that was once essential and nourished us. The priority and emphasis are on individuality, respect for one an-

other, the intellectual affinities necessary for shared plans, and the lovely time spent together when it is what both want.

In love, because of this dependence, the partners live in each other's pockets. In relationships between very different people, this necessarily means the hegemony of one over the other and the concessions that the "weaker" one makes. The "weaker" one is actually the strongest, but this isn't the place to go into the complex dynamics of these couples. The tension and fights are constant; tears are spilled regularly. Love is thus, above all, a source of suffering and pain.

Even in the much rarer cases in which there is fusion between like-minded people (after a story of passionate love with a happy ending), in which being together all the time happens almost spontaneously, unexpected and highly disturbing worries can arise. The greatest is the fear of disappointing one's partner. Since love is derived from admiration, if there is disappointment there will be less admiration, which may raise doubts as to the continuity of the love. In other words, those who have intense relationships like this feel very threatened, having to behave in accordance with their lover's expectations in order to keep deserving the blessing of their love. A second threat is thus created — as if the fear of happiness were not enough!

**This demanding atmosphere is incredibly tiring. Before we were talking about the fights between people who were together because of their differences;**

now it is brutal intimate pressure. It's hard to say which is worse. The partners feel as if they are under constant threat and that they might lose their lover in the most terrible way; that they may no longer be the object of their love. They feel as if they are being continually assessed, given a proficiency exam every day, as if yesterday's assessment weren't valid for today — hence the need to repeat words like "I love you" and pledge eternal love over and over.

Good quality relationships, characterized by reciprocal feelings and greater affinities, can be quite difficult precisely due to the seriousness with which all matters related to the character and behaviour of each are treated. In relationships between opposites, there is an atmosphere of tolerance, at least on the part of the generous. The selfish one is more demanding, but the focus is on practical aspects of life in common. They don't tend to make demands of an intellectual — much less moral — nature.

It is no wonder that bilateral love inspires great growth. The pressures are so intense that there is no other solution but to overcome one's limits so as not to disappoint one's lover. There is a great deal of personal growth: intellectual, emotional, and moral. What is happening? Their individuality is reappearing! The positive assessment that one lover receives from the other (the person whose opinion matters most), reinforces and reaffirms their self-esteem. The reward for their effort is that their fear of letting the other one down gradually

wanes. Graduation day comes: the approval is definitive and unconditional.

From this day on, the graduates explore their individuality with less and less fear that this might mean losing their partner. The phenomenon is reciprocal, such that, through trial and error and several false starts, they manage to break the symbiotic dependence. It becomes clear that the other ingredients — friendship, sex, shared plans — are more than enough to keep the relationship alive. It not only survives the destruction of fusion, but it gains a richness and cheer that were buried by the lifestyle typical of those who love one another and think they "only need each other"! We have reached the terrain of love+.

(I would like to make an observation about something that intrigues me: our very first cell comes from the fusion of an egg cell and a sperm cell, both incomplete; these "halves" unite to form a single cell and generate a new life. It is as if we retrace this same path in adult life: we feel incomplete although we're not, and we meld with another human being in an alliance that we have learned to call love. Reciprocal pressure gains such force that it takes us in the opposite direction, such that we manage to complete the process of individuation. Our companion on this journey, which ultimately gives rise to two whole individuals, is the object of our love+.)

Love+ has a spirit of freedom and respect. The need to prove something to one's partner disappears, and this extends, at least partially, to other people. The benefits

to one's individuality are very relevant. The inevitable differences in the way the lovers behave and think are no longer seen as threatening: they are not a reason for disappointment, nor do they pose a threat to the stability of the relationship, which they now feel is solid enough to allow for long "solo" flights.

Concessions are minimal, and the way each one lives is similar to the life they would choose if they lived alone. In love+, people's day-to-day lives are not unlike the lives of those who decide to live alone. For those who like to have a steady partner for sex and company in their leisure time, there are only advantages! This is the reign of trust, since more individuated people are also intellectually honest, loyal, and sincere. There is no place for any kind of betrayal or for actions that break the pact between the two.

## thirty six

**I would like to suggest** a possibility that, while unlikely, could always happen. Couples in relationships between opposites, who (when they familiarize themselves with the vision of relationships that I defend in this book) become aware of the need to reassess the nature of the relationship they have built, may make efforts to do so. As long as the feeling that brought them together — more intense on the part of the generous — is alive, there is always time to rethink the path they have taken. The wear and tear on the relationship tends to be less in the first few years as well as in cases in which there is less distance from the point of equilibrium.

I have already said that there are degrees of selfishness and generosity, such that most of us who belong to one of these two groups are not extreme cases. We are not anti-social beings, nor are we martyrs or saints. As a rule, we seek partners who are as far from the point of equilibrium as ourselves, each in the opposite direction. The desire to grow towards fairness may be present in both, as both generosity and selfishness are a form of moral immaturity and give rise to inner dissatisfaction.

There must be real bilateral willingness and the partners need to be able to change the relationship. **This will have to be based on sincerity: all of their dissatisfactions must be aired objectively and without being afraid of hurting the other person (in the case of the generous one) or losing privileges (in the case of the selfish one). Both must be willing to subject themselves to sincere and deep self-criticism, which always implies suffering.** They will have to undo the thesis that there is a villain and a victim, and both will have to assume equal shares of responsibility for having built a relationship around so many subtle and tiring intrigues.

**The most important thing is the sincere desire to change.** Both partners will have to commit to try, together, to move towards individuality and building a relationship that respects the differences of each. It isn't easy, but it is possible that these couples, who came together because of their fear of love, manage to progress towards love+. They may realize that, in many aspects, it is easier than romantic fusion, which is demanding and sometimes suffocating. **Because love+ respects individuality, it may be less threatening, especially for the more selfish sorts, who are so fearful of fusion.**

I consider intellectual honesty, loyalty, and the desire to establish a relationship based on deep friendship to be the fundamental factors required to embark on this difficult undertaking. I also think that, perhaps in the not-so-distant future, young people will work harder to establish their individuality before getting into committed relationships. This may create conditions that help shorten the long path to overcoming love and its regressive nature.

I don't believe in insurmountable obstacles. We can make efforts to grow at any age and in any circumstances. The difficulties are almost always big for all of us. However, I can't think of a more important task than trying, every day, to become fairer and more prepared to live a happy life.

# 37

thirty seven

**There is no doubt** in my mind that love+ is much more consistent with happiness than any manifestation of love, be it fantasy, unilateral, or bilateral symbiotic love. Dependency means concessions; and concessions, annoyance. When I think about happiness, I always take into consideration a certain inevitable quota of suffering and limitations on one's freedom — which we have to get through as quickly as possible. I think of real limitations that have to do with the commitments we make out of necessity or voluntarily; not the ones that aren't obligatory, which give rise to unnecessary frustration and pain.

It is essential that we sort unpleasant activities into two groups: the obligatory ones (such as the funeral of someone important in our lives, hospital visits, certain family events, etc.) and the optional ones (like going to an opera, going out with acquaintances we don't find particularly interesting, taking trips we don't want to, etc.). We shouldn't avoid the obligatory ones, which are part of the rituals of civility of the culture we live in. My view of the optional ones is very different. This is because doing something our lover wants us to means allowing ourselves to be irritated; that is, someone will always be put out, which makes it a bad solution. Additionally, when we make concessions beyond our quota we always end up fighting, which is a way of avenging ourselves of the pressure we are feeling. No one is so saintly that they are above this.

**The possessiveness and jealousy typical of dependence in a relationship are an inexorable source of suffering, reciprocal torture and undue limitations on people's rights to come and go as they please. They are not compatible with happiness and do not evolve as the years go by. As long as there is dependence there will be the need to control the person on whom one depends.** We will only manage to eliminate jealousy and possessiveness by eliminating love (the explicit objective of this book), which undermines ideals of happiness, emotional growth, and freedom. These things are only compatible with the full expression of individuality.

**Friendship is a positive pleasure, a permanent and renewable source of joy, wellbeing, and happiness. The same is valid for sex (when it is a source of pleasure and not tied up with games of power, seduction, and domination), intellectual pleasures, and the full expression of individual freedom.** The quality of life of people pejoratively referred to as solitary (could it be envy?) and those who have love+ is compatible with the state of serenity and the greatest possible number of happy moments that, together, characterize what I call happiness.

**Happiness depends on emotional and moral maturity. It doesn't come from an easy formula, of the kind that one finds in the manuals that periodically infest bookshop shelves.** I don't have — nor do I ever hope to — a talent for tricking people, so I can only state my belief: **happiness is possible, but it requires great effort, individual growth, patience, and determination.**

The number of happy people may be small. But it may change and this state may come to be accessible to everyone, at least if we consider that emotional maturity (competence at overcoming frustration), the ability to live alone or in good company, and the enjoyment of physical and intellectual pleasures are its main ingredients. This is completely different to associating happiness with material wealth, extraordinary beauty, and fame. The world of the rich, beautiful, and famous is, by definition, limited. If we consider it to be the most relevant, we condemn the overwhelming majority of human beings to unhappiness. Such aristocratic properties are highly valued in our culture. This is, in my opinion, a huge mistake against which we should protest vehemently.

**I am only interested in democratic possibilities, those that could one day be part of the lives of most people. My vision of love+ belongs to this context. The death of fusion is part of the democratic happy ending that, without deluding anyone or lying about possible obstacles and the length of the journey, has guided all of my intellectual work.**

# thirty eight

**The path described** here is part of the itinerary of an explorer. It has been travelled by those who strive to better understand the phenomenon of love and haven't been able to draw from the experience of reliable ancestors. Just like in the centuries before us, for most people love is still a big enigma, something indecipherable. It is a source of suffering (considered worthy, proof that one has been part of something true and sincere). Those whose love is real must suffer the pain of a possible separation; they must live with the uncertainty of not knowing if they are loved in return; they must quake with jealousy at the thought of being left for someone else.

I have never agreed with this point of view. I have always thought that love was an emotion that deserved to be better understood and assessed from all angles. In my mind, a good emotion is one that brings happiness, peace, stability, and trust. I have gone through various phases in the last forty years, in which I have studied and sought to understand everything I can on the subject. **I am now convinced that the love we know is immature and regressive. Therefore, I am against what is treated as the most beautiful and sublime emotion.**

If the choice is between love and individuality, I choose the latter. I do this knowing that it implies the death of romantic love, which I believe to be the great villain of history. The ending is happy because it brings an end to useless and wearisome suffering. Freed from the desire for fusion (which I understand to be something from the past, not the future), individuals can walk the path towards autonomy and freedom. They free themselves for once and for all of the obsession of having to find someone to depend on or who depends on them. People have always sought reciprocal dependence to lessen the inexorable feeling of forsakenness. When everything is fine, they feel cosiness and peace; when there is some kind of disagreement, the bad feeling comes back and people will make any kind of concession to save the relationship and gain temporary peace, at least until the next falling out.

Cosiness is perhaps our first and most serious dependence, an addiction and a vicious circle without an exit. I don't see a big difference between relationship dependence and other kinds of addiction, whether cigarettes, alcohol, marijuana, or so many other drugs and situations. I have been comparing love to addiction since the 1970's and discussed it in one of my earliest works. Love isn't all that noble or wise, nor does it deserve the worship in verse and prose that it has always received.

I think the repetitive and monotonous insistence of artists on describing every last detail of the same love stories means they haven't managed to decipher its enigmas. I don't consider this a sign of the importance of love, rather, that we are not doing very well in this area. **We tend to neglect what is going well and worry about what is in dire straights. A couple that is happy in love, with a regular, satisfying sex life, will think less about the subject than those who are having problems. Our culture's obsession with love — and sex — indicates that these matters continue to intrigue and are poorly resolved.**

Throughout the second half of the 20th century, many of the best minds put their cards on the revolutionary potential of sexual liberation. They imagined that sexually free people, happy with their multiple experiences would be more solidary, less consumerist, more aligned with humanistic ideals. They were wrong. This so-called sexual emancipation stepped up competition and stimulated the game of seduction in its malevolent version: rivalry between the sexes and over-preoccupation with physical appearances and wealth. In short, everything got worse — and how!

**We need the humility to recognize that the idea was wrong: sexual liberation will have taken place when people are no longer obsessed with the subject, rather than placing it on a pedestal.** The same thing goes for love, which competes with sex for the primacy of being the subject that is most on people's minds. We will have made progress as regards relationships when we dedicate less time to them, which is impossible, since love is rich in repetitive surprises. Salvation is pointing the finger at the nature of the feeling we call love. We need to stop insisting, trying to make such a childish manifestation work in adult life.

The victory of individualism is similar to recovering from any kind of addiction. We suffer a lot in the beginning at the idea that we have to be self-sufficient and get by on our own; but as time goes by we remember the drug — or the relationship dependence — less and less. Feelings of forsakenness are alleviated when we confront them directly, without resorting to romantic palliatives — or drugs. The inevitable residues show that we haven't managed to free ourselves completely of our early experiences. (In the book *Cigarro: um adeus possível* [Cigarettes: a Possible Goodbye] I draw a clear parallel between the phenomenon of love and addictions. In it I argue that cigarettes substitute pacifiers, the first addiction of most; and pacifiers, as we know, take the place of the mother!)

When we manage to free ourselves of emotional dependence, we gain a lot in terms of self-esteem. It is an accomplishment we are proud of for having had the strength to face and overcome an enormous obstacle. We suffer, it is true; but it is a constructive pain that leads to growth and freedom. The pain of love is repetitive, useless, and unproductive, because it doesn't go anywhere.

When free people with good self-esteem establish relationships, they do so because of their intellectual affinities. Emotional and moral growth is essential and present in everyone who has managed to approach the condition of *fair* (overcoming the selfishness and generosity that define relationships between opposites). Reciprocal trust and respect determine a more consistent and constructive relationship. **I call the feeling that unites free people "love+", bearing in mind what the word "love" has meant to people.** Love+ is closer to friendship than traditional love and is optional, since free people have no problems being alone.

If my considerations in this book are reasonably accurate, I think they can help us a lot. **A social order that stimulates individualism — and an adequate approach to education — may help shorten the path described here. Courage is needed to change the focus in this direction, although this is already happening due to technological advances. Nowadays, however, we are living a kind of "supervised" individualism: we are freer than ever before, but radically manipulated by the media and publicity.**

The balance is dubious, and I think that this manipulation may begin to lose its power in the near future. Independent people with good self-esteem can rebel more easily and start to think for themselves. Untangling the knot related to the issue of love creates the conditions dreamed of by the idealists of last century. It creates the conditions for benevolent, free, fair people to think more seriously about building a community life founded on ideals of freedom and justice.

**Societies are human agglomerates. Only fair people can build a fairer society. As for the future, I**

**Flávio Gikovate**

think a lot about artists: what will they think, what will they write about when they are no longer busy deciphering the enigmas of love and sex? What will their paintings be like? What music will they compose? We may see a leap in quality that we haven't for a long time. We may have the chance to, as a species, continue existing and progressing towards things we still haven't been able to imagine. At any rate, we will be replacing our obsession with the past with the desire to discover what is yet to come.

IMPRESSO NA
**sumago** gráfica editorial ltda
rua itauna, 789  vila maria
**02111-031**  são paulo  sp
telefax 11 **2955 5636**
**sumago**@terra.com.br